Dla Bogus.—

 # SOCCER

THE FIRST-BALL GAME

by Martin Bidzinski

1 szacunkiem

J/Bidzinski

REEDSWAIN
PUBLISHING

Library of Congress
Cataloging - in - Publication Data

Soccer: The First Ball Game
by Martin Bidzinski

ISBN-13: 978-1-59164-260-2
ISBN-10: 1-59164-260-4
© 2022

Art Direction, Layout and Proofing
Bryan R. Beaver

Diagrams created with
easySportsGraphics
www.sports-graphics.com

Reedswain Publishing
88 Wells Road
Spring City, PA 19475
www. reedswain.com
orders@reedswain.com

Cover Illustrations
Players:©michalsanca/Adobe Stock
Ball: ©calima/Adobe Stock

TABLE OF CONTENTS

INTRODUCTION

Nothing in the game of life is unrelated to the game of soccer, not when there are people involved. It is a mistake to believe that the development of any young player to play the game of soccer based on the first-ball game has anything to do about changing how the game is played, especially at the professional level of the game. In reality, a player who is developed with the first-ball game in mind will be a skillful player who can be effective at any club, playing any style. Sometimes the way the game is played is down to the manager of the club, and this can be based on any number of practical objectives. My work, therefore, is always about the development of young players in a way that would enable them to play soccer to the first-ball game level and adapt to any level should the need arise. In recent times the way the game is played is defined as either "First-ball game" or "Second-ball game". In this book I will explain the difference between the two from a player development point of view.

THE LONG ROAD INTO THE PROFESSIONAL GAME

The game of soccer is no different from any other human endeavor. In many countries, the journey into the professional game is haphazard to say the least. It begins within the school environment, where children as young as nine years of age can represent the school team. From there, the progression into the next level could see any of them given the opportunity to represent the local town team. Should the player catch the eye, so to speak, at the town team level, this then could lead to more opportunities, such as being selected to play for the regional team. When the player plays for the regional team, this could then open the door for the player to be selected to represent the country at youth level and so on. If a player makes it into their country's representative Under 21 team, he is now in the position of attracting interest from Professional Soccer Clubs. What happens in the school environment level runs side by side with Private Soccer clubs, who mostly have an interest in players up to the age of twelve to sixteen. What happens at that level depends on the Private Club's connections with a professional club. If a club is interested in a player that plays for the Private Club, that player may be invited to the professional club for training at a young age. Once that happens, the player could well be playing for the club up to the age of eighteen, when he is either retained or discarded. Professional soccer is big business, and as such there are many factors that may come into play to block a player, talented or otherwise, from making any further progress into the higher ranks of the game. For example, in many cases the people in charge of the first team in a professional soccer club will not even look at a player if he/she is not represented by an agent.

THE CHANCE LOTTERY

Everything depends on circumstances. Some of the professional soccer clubs in the lower divisions of the league don't even run a youth development academy, claiming they can't afford to do so. In reality, they don't do it because they know they can run the first team with players who have been discarded by the bigger clubs. If any player makes it from this long road of player development, it's because they are obviously competent enough to come through, yet even here it would mostly be on the basis of being fit for the "horses for courses" agenda (big and strong), which is a selection criteria that lends itself to the second-ball game.

CHAPTER ONE

UNDERSTANDING THE REALITY

There are few managers in the world of professional soccer who have the understanding or the aspiration to play the first-ball game, which is a phrase conveniently sidelined by those who ply their trade on the back of the "big and strong" player. How many managers in the world of soccer actually have a 'hands on' approach to the development of any young player? How many of them actually know or care what the first-ball game is all about? Or about what kind of training they should use to make the distinction between the first and second-ball game? One of their responsibilities is to talk to the media, hence many of them talk a good game in front of the camera but have very little hands-on coaching ability at the training ground, especially when it comes to the youth side of the game. In fact, even at the youth development level, how many of the youth coaches distinguish the work between the first-ball game elements and the second-ball game elements? Not many, because they don't know what that difference is. How many youth coaches know what work is related to the promotion of the second-ball game and what training actually promotes the development of the first-ball game? From the school environment up to the professional level many of the coaches support the second-ball game without knowing any difference. Do they know what a proper first touch really is, never mind how to teach it? How many of them could care less because, as far as they are concerned, there is no difference from a playing point of view. At many professional clubs, the job of the manager is to look after the interest of the first team, which in many cases means getting the coaches to dumb things down because they are following the "Horses for Courses" ideology of the second-ball game.

THE MEDIA PUNDITS

The media pundits use a language that is complicit with a second-ball game mentality. As a result, many coaches think that a team like Barcelona plays their game based on two touch soccer, when technically speaking this is not the case. The influential language of the pundits talks up the second-ball game and fails to highlight the lack of "two-footedness" in top players. How many coaches think that this is even a problem? Bad influences result in bad coaching practices. Some think it is possible to solve the problem of a lack of two-footedness by conditioning the player to have a go playing the ball with the weak foot. Another myth believed by most coaches is that developing a good first touch to the ball can be achieved by conditioning the player to take two contacts with the ball. From a technical point of view, placing conditions on what foot to use or the number of touches in training is a total misrepresentation of the ability to take a meaningful first touch to the ball, one that can make it the most effective in terms of possession. But then again, why bother with such details when the name of the game for many is not about skillful players keeping possession of the ball, but about hoofing the ball down the field and relying on the battling attributes of big and strong players to win the second ball? As a result, we can see a lack of technical progress in many soccer playing countries. There are many reasons for a lack of progress, but the most obvious of them are as follows:-

(A)   Most coaches use second-ball game training methods without knowing any differently.

(B)   Many coaches support the "horses for courses" mentality

(C)   "Toeing the line" means having an anti-first-ball game approach to the proper development of players based on the first-ball game

(D)   Many of the conventional training sessions don't actually represent the divisions between the work that relates to the first-ball game (fast and slow twitch muscle orientations) and the work that relates to the second-ball game (slow twitch muscle orientations)

(E)   The divisions between fitness for fitness sake (second-ball game) and fitness for having the ability to play the first-ball game is missing from most coaching systems.

HOW SIMPLE CAN IT BE?

A training session that applies fragments from the game as a means of development, or even the simple act of playing soccer in it's different forms (for example five-a-sides, etc) may seem purposeful from a development point of view, but actually prevents many young players from fulfilling their true potential. This is because in many cases the training objectives are not detailed enough to make the distinction between what type of development (physical or psychological) is actually taking place at the different levels of the game. Let me give you an example of a reality in the game today that illustrates the need to understand the difference between proper development and no development through enforced conventional thinking. In the English Premiership we have teams like Everton and teams like Manchester City. I have analyzed a game recently played between the two clubs. Everton is a team that has obviously been created with deals for players and not on any first-ball game coaching manual. The agents' hands are all over this team. They have simply made deals on players without any knowledge of compatibility between the players and this has ended with a bag of all sorts. In other words, a team of players who are incompatible with each other are incapable of playing the first-ball game.

STUCK IN THE SECOND-BALL GAME

THE NECESSARY ADAPTATIONS BY THE MANAGERS

In many cases, when a manager comes into a club, he takes the job and runs the club in a way that suits the players he has available. There are many reasons why the club can stay where it is or move up or down the ladder. The worst-case scenario is when a club has the money to buy players, but have no idea or concern about compatibility issues. An incoming manager will have to adapt to what he has in front of him. The Everton manager during the 2021 season clearly adapted to the reality of the club. The most obvious of adaptations can be seen around the Everton goalkeeper, who naturally kicks the long ball. The manager keeps the long ball kicker because the players at his disposal lack the necessary skills to build the attack from the back with possession. Out of necessity, he is more than happy to implement the second-ball game. Such an approach shores up the cracks, but sooner or later all managers that find themselves in such a reality will fail to deliver on expectations.

IN COMPARISON

It is more than obvious that the Manchester City team is built around a procurement policy which has nothing to do with the youth side of the game. However, the procurement of players at Manchester City is one that is based on a greater understanding of compatibility and therefore of what to bring into the club. It is obvious that at City this is not simply a question of making deals on players and the Devil may care. It is possible to note that players are compatible with each other, the meaning of which is not understood by many who pretend they know what that is. The compatibility has to be based on the quality of the player from a technical and physical point of view.

THE ANTI-HORSES FOR COURSES WORKING SOLUTIONS

My 'Youth Player Development System', based on the lateral concept, changes the way the game is played. Challenging the "horses for courses" objectives is my goal when it comes to the development of young players. The way the game is played can be down to the philosophy of the manager and this can be down to the needs of the club, set by all sorts of problems related to the game. Most of what takes place at the professional level of the game has nothing to do with Youth Development or how the first team plays. Some clubs can afford to procure players based on the manager's philosophy, most can't. Manchester City manager Pep Guardiola is one that clearly believes in keeping possession of the ball. Fortunately for him, this playing philosophy is supported by the club and City obviously has the money to support it. And what exactly is that playing philosophy? How does Guardiola want his team to play the game? The answer to this became clear with the very first move he made when he arrived. The first thing Guardiola did was to change the goalkeeper from one that kicked the long ball to one that was comfortable playing the ball out from the back. Why? Because he clearly believes in keeping possession of the ball and playing the first-ball game.

THE LACK OF TALENT

Manchester City buy the best players from around the world. At City they don't look for players who come from the 'Second-ball game' environment because they know that sticking to the local 'Horses For Courses' mentality fails to produce skillful players. It should be more than obvious that the development of a player depends on what happens at youth level. It should also be obvious that the input to the development of a player is consequential.

FROM A DIFFERENT CULTURE

The Manchester City goalkeeper, just like so many of their players, happens to come from a country where the game is based on a more skillful mentality and this can be said to represent a different approach to player development, one where the coaches aspire to the reality of the first-ball game (Possession Soccer). The lack of development, on the other hand, can be seen in the reality of the Everton goalkeeper, who represents a country which has a cold approach to the skillful side of the game and so is a representative of one that simply supports an agenda which is set in the second-ball game mentality. The difference between the two goalkeepers can be said to be a way of playing that suits the needs of the club.

THE REALITY

There are 92 clubs in English Soccer Leagues, most of them semi-professional. Many of the clubs, therefore, operate a 'Horses For Courses' agenda, for many reasons. A lot of countries in the world copy the English way of working. In general terms 'Youth development' is of little concern to these clubs. What clubs get up to in the name of their vested interests has nothing to do with young players. Absolutely nothing! Why do you think many countries fail to win the World Cup? Failure to do so comes from the reality of what happens at youth level and even from what they coach at the professional club level. It is not difficult to keep the game ticking over for purpose, not when there is an abundance of players who, mostly through circumstance, have a second-ball game capability. Most professional clubs stay afloat financially by any means necessary. Some of the top clubs hope their brand name will pull them through the bad times. The application of the principle called 'Horses For Courses' is one that keeps everything going, just. Most supporters of the game of soccer have no idea about what the 'Horses For Courses' mentality is all about. Most players develop their ability by playing or practicing fragments of the game known as "drills". This type of work is supported with fitness training throughout their playing career. What level they reach depends on their aptitude to the game.

MOST CERTAINLY IN THE SCHOOL ENVIRON-MENT

The school environment teaches the children to be 'Jacks Of All Trades' but 'Masters' of not that much. Only after leaving the school environment can anyone dedicate their time and specialize in what they want to achieve. When it comes to soccer, most children don't spend enough time on the game to become 'Masters Of the Game'. Playing soccer now and then, even if they get the chance to work on and practice fragments of the game, is never enough. Coaches begrudgingly point to players like Lionel Messi and George Best, conveniently forgetting that both players spent a lot of time with the ball at their feet up to the age of fourteen. Of course Messi stands out when he is playing against players who come with a second-ball game capability. Everything is hidden from the reality because when it comes to the professional game everything can be shored up by a selection criteria known as 'Big & Strong'. In other words, there is no need to worry about player development as such and they can afford to poo-poo any worthwhile coaching message because they choose the big and strong 'Men' that can run and kick a ball, which will always cover the needs of most clubs. There is no need for skillful players because able men can play the game to a middle of the road standard everywhere, which is mostly 'Second-ball game' orientated or 'Hybrid' at best.

CHAPTER TWO

THE PLAYING PHILOSOPHY

I hope that youth coaches will not follow the 'Horses for Courses' ideology, but instead embrace a philosophy that is relevant to actual player development. There is a need for special training solutions going forward because as things stand everything is geared towards the second-ball game capability based on the big and strong players. There are forces at work outside of the training environment that, unless checked, have massive consequences for the development of young players. The real development of a player does not start with any playing philosophy as such. There are many influences on human development that are almost set in stone. In fact, sometimes things are so entrenched that it takes years to unravel from a proper development point of view. All humans are creatures of habits that result from the set rules governing the social order. In the not too distant past and even now, religious beliefs have influenced how people should behave and develop. An example is the frowned upon use of the left hand, which is said to be the 'Devil's hand'. The "devil's hand" idea is probably the most influential idea of all that is related to human development and has had its obvious consequences to sport as a whole and soccer in particular.

THE INADEQUATE CONSEQUENCES

It is a fact of life that all physical actions, no matter how insignificant, develop muscle memory. If all physical actions are dominated by the right hand, almost everyone develops limitations of one form or another, such as the under-development of the right side of the brain. Such facts are now out in the open because science recognizes that the right hand is controlled by the left side of the brain, and vice versa. It is difficult to imagine the consequential realities of even such a simple analysis, until you accept that all physical actions generated by the body are instigated by signals coming from the brain. The signals from the brain go to the parts of the body that are required to be moved, hence the 'Muscle Memory' development can only take place where the signal from the brain goes for any physical movement to take place. Nobody questions the physical effects of the use of the right hand or of any forward-moving action on the development of the human being and yet such things are actually significant to the development of every human being, long before any artificial input comes into play. Forbidding people to use the left hand has led to the development of the right side of the physical body at the expense of the left, which can be seen in the obvious reality that most people are weaker and less capable on the left side of the body. An indirect consequence of this is the lack of collaboration between the left and right side of the brain. This impacts on the development of any young soccer player and if not checked will most certainly lead to a second-ball game capability.

THE CHANGING REALITY

Top drawer professional soccer clubs play the first-ball game (the skillful game of soccer). Adapt or be left behind. What many coaches fail to see is that the progressive development of the human race will not come from the use of the right hand only, nor will it come from the existing forward-moving mentality. Expanding the intellect of the human being can only come from the application of another working dimension, the lateral dimension, which is as yet not fully understood by many who work with young players. As with all things new, it is not easy to implement the lateral dimension into everything human beings do, but its very existence is already in place. It is right in front of us, even if many of us don't see it.

THE LATERAL DIMENSION

To counter the negative influential forces on development, you need to specialize. In other words, coaches have to implement working solutions that counter the one handed/footed, forward-moving world. The first-ball game is achieved by working with lateral forms in the development process. In my training concept I have a foundational nine cone placement form, for example, that changes everything and is very consequential because it is the lateral physical movements within this form that automatically target the development of a higher intellect and physical ability. The lateral movements affect and develop both the right and the left side of the brain in equal measure, and within that reality comes a greater improvement in physical and mental capability.

NOT A DEVELOPMENT FORM

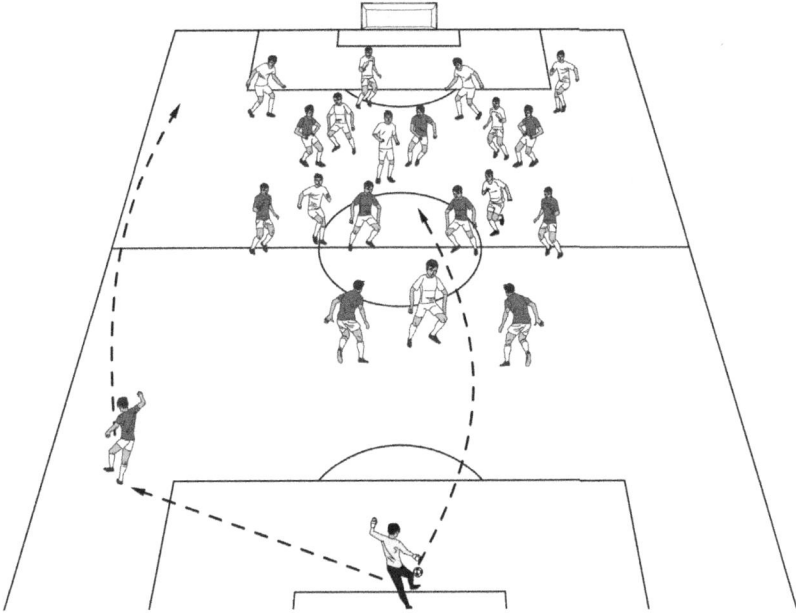

THE LONG BALL GAME – A SECOND-BALL GAME MENTALITY

When all is said and done, there is a constant in place that will never change - all forms of input into the development of the human being are quickly established in the muscle memory bank with practice, but what kind of practice will always be consequential. The progressive way forward, therefore, is to work on and develop the brain as a single unifying unit. The collaboration between the left and right side of the brain can only be achieved by working on the physical movements that adhere to the lateral dimension and not to the forward-moving reality that all human beings have had to work with since the beginning of time. In this example, the goalkeeper kicks the long ball into the mix, the "mix" being players pack the midfield area to await the long ball kick out. In the above scenario, which underpins the second-ball game, nothing skillful comes to mind, only the battling efforts to try to win possession of the ball. The above example is useful to chapter three of this book.

CHAPTER THREE

THE ENERGY FACTOR

The first-ball game is based on the concept known as the pass and move game. This reference is a little misleading however, because the pass of the ball can be played to any distance. The better way to describe the first-ball game is actually to state that it is based on sharing possession of the ball and therefore reliant more on the short pass, one that is played to feet, often in tight spaces. The long ball game is obviously different in terms of the physical energy requirement. Running in straight lines requires power based on the slow twitch muscle forms, whereas the first-ball game requires power that comes from the fast twitch muscles. Running in straight lines is not as difficult as short bursts of pace, which require kinetic energy. How this type of energy is created is one of the aims of lateral development training.

WHAT KIND OF ENERGY

If you don't understand how the body creates energy, you will not be able to make the distinction in training between work that is directly related to the second-ball game and that which is related to the first-ball game. The most common understanding to date is that carbohydrates create energy. However, transferring carbs into energy is not the only way it is created. The lateral forms on player development also produce energy. Hence, when it comes to being physically capable, it is not just about the food we eat. Oddly enough, sometimes a lack of energy comes from the food we eat. Nutrition is consequential on the body in many respects. Eating meat, for example, starves the whole of the body of oxygen, because the oxygen is used up in the digestive process. All too often we see a soccer player lying on the ground, with cramped legs up in the air. This is the reality of oxygen starvation in the muscles of the leg.

CREATING ENERGY – THE SIMPLIFIED VERSION

The most common of foods consumed everywhere in the world is bread. When we eat bread, here is what happens.

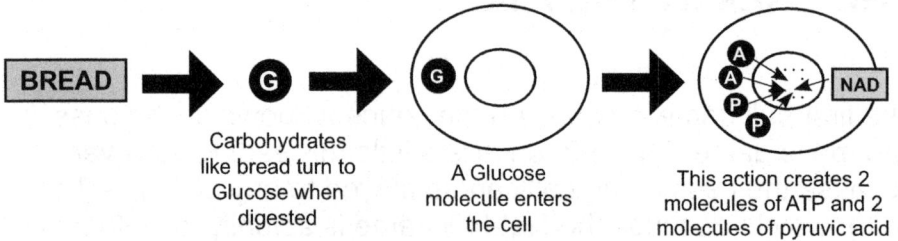

Carbohydrates like bread turn to Glucose when digested

A Glucose molecule enters the cell

This action creates 2 molecules of ATP and 2 molecules of pyruvic acid

CREATING ENERGY

The process of creating energy, other than stored energy that is, also uses oxygen, so here is a simple but relevant version of what happens when we eat and how what we eat impacts our ability to perform a physical task. In the above diagrams we see the four molecules enter into the 'Mitochondria', which is located on the inside of the cell and one electron carrier called NAD (NICODIN-EMIDE ADENINE DINUCLEOTIDE) joins them – at which point carbon dioxide is released. This is the Aerobic (oxygen based) cellular respiration. The end product of this cell respiration cycle is the coveted molecule called ATP (ADENOSINE TRIPHOSPHATE) – The molecule ATP is essential for muscle contraction, without which the body could not function. Any excess energy is stored around the muscle in the form of creatine phosphate, or CP. This inner source of energy can sustain contraction for up to 15 seconds and does not require oxygen.

ATP = THE ULTIMATE DRIVING ENGINE FOR MUSCLE CONTRACTION

The above greatly simplified starting points are foundational to the next piece of the puzzle, which is understanding the function and composition of the muscle.

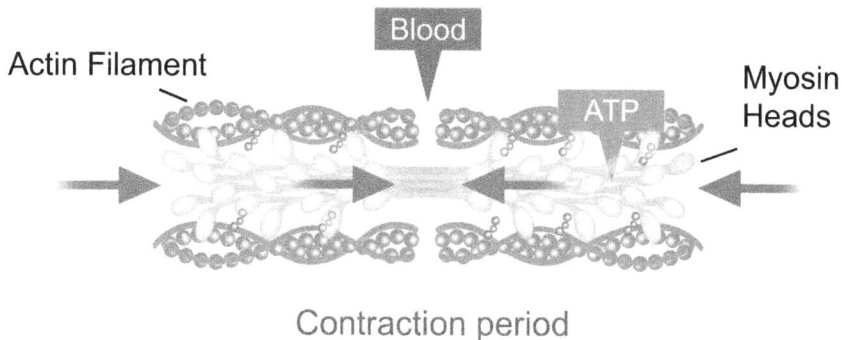

Contraction period

The muscle is made up of fast and slow twitch muscle bundles, which are constructed with filaments known as Actin and Myosin. The Actin and Myosin filaments are moved by employing the ATP molecule energy source that is generated in the Mitochondrion. What happens on a micro biological level is that in order to contract the muscle fibers to move a limb, the Myosin heads pop up and attach themselves to the actin filament.

The Myosin heads then pull on the actin filament and this action in turn contracts the muscle and moves the limb. This happens by virtue of the muscle having connective tissues attached to the required limb.

THE SIGNAL FROM THE BRAIN TO ANY MOTOR UNIT

The decision to move a limb is communicated from the brain through the spine in a process known as asynchronous stimulation. The basic requirements of physical movement happen in a state of Aerobic Respiration, which uses oxygen. These are slow twitch muscle forms. They contain lots of Mitochondria and are useful for power play and therefore to the second-ball game requirements predominantly. The 'Fast Twitch' Muscle Forms have relatively fewer Mitochondria in them because they don't use oxygen in cell respiration. This is a general representation of the composition of a muscle form in order to make the distinction between the reality that slow twitch muscles exist alongside fast twitch muscles, which is important from a physical development point of view.

THE COMPOSITION OF THE MUSCLES CAN BE CHANGED BY THE LEVEL OF EFFORT MADE ON THEM

THIS IS CALLED - ENTROPHY

When muscles undergo intense exercise, as from resistance training, there is trauma to the muscle. When muscle cells are damaged this is mended by cell organelles called satellite cells, which are located on the outside of the muscle (between the basal lamina and the plasma membrane) that keeps the muscle bundles in place.

In essence, a biological effort to repair or replace damaged muscle begins with the satellite cells fusing together to the damaged muscle. This action repeated leads to increases in muscle cross sectional area of hypertrophy.

Note -The satellite cells have only the one nucleus but can replicate by dividing.

As the satellite cells multiply, some remain as organelles on the muscle, whereas, the majority mature into normal cells and fuse to other cells to form new muscle strands. In this process the myofibrils (the Actin and Myosin filaments) will increase in thickness and number.

RELEVANT TO THE GAME OF SOCCER

Any signal from the brain to a muscle is not accidental. It is based FIRST OF ALL on the bank of memory in the brain allotted to a specific physical movement learned. A signal from the brain for a muscle to function for purpose goes to the appropriate muscle bundle. Which bundles are used is dependent on the physical effort required for that movement. If, for example, the physical action is sedentary and the breathing pattern is normal, in the sense that nothing much is going on and the participant is not out of breath, this is the aerobic state, in which the slow twitch muscle fibers come into play. On the other hand, if the physical action is explosive for any length of time and the athlete runs out of oxygen, this is the Anaerobic state, where cell respiration is internal and the fast twitch muscles come into play. All forms of training have their consequences on the development of the human being. Every physical exertion has its consequences. Unfortunately, there are vested interests in the second-ball game that ignore any notion of a scientific approach to any soccer endeavor. Most problems are "solved" by lots of running and weight training. The attitude to the game of soccer is deliberately backward to a point that some in the game refer to the scientific approach as, and I quote, "Are you into them naughts and crosses?". Such attitudes exist and obviously nobody questions them. Unfortunately, it's easy to get away with it because it is not that difficult to keep the 'Second-Ball Game' alive with drills, running and lots of slogans such as 'Just let them play'.

THE HARSH REALITY

It is fair to say that a lot of things have changed, but also worth remembering that it was not all that long ago that a damaged foot was mended by giving the unfortunate player a bucket filled with water and ice, sitting them down outside in the corridor, away from the dressing room with his foot in the bucket. Of course, things have gotten better, for those who can afford it. There are lots of clubs in the lower divisions of the game that even now rely on outside help should an injury take place. The worst thing that I have noted even now when a player is injured is that you see the physio giving the player a pain killing tablet. Don't they realize that dumbing down the pain could even cause more harm than good. So have times really changed all that much?

CHAPTER FOUR

NOT A CLOSED MIND SET

I have spent all my life in sporting endeavors for the love of sport and obviously not for the money. I played soccer and even managed a couple of professional clubs. I also played the game of snooker, where my highest break was 95, I now play the game of golf in my free time, but my main passion and time has always been dedicated to soccer. All of the above experiences combined have not been a waste of time, because all that I experienced gave me the understanding of the consequential reality that comes from the forward-moving world and its consequences on the human being from a developmental point of view.

THE OBVIOUS DIRECTION OF PLAY

The forward-moving mentality is wired into the human brain. When most people watch a game of soccer, all they see is the direction of play, which to them is obviously forward. The forward-moving direction of play has not changed in the majority of soccer clubs in the world. However, we now live at a time when this forward-moving reality is not the only reality in the game and things are beginning to change. I am lucky to see a country like Spain, for example, make the progressive leap in soccer and embrace a different reality to that of the 'Forward-moving Game'. In England, while we still have entrenched views, we do have clubs like Brentford, Brighton and Leeds United, newly promoted into the English Premiership that also buck the trend and employ a multi directional game, which is the first-ball game.

THE SECOND-BALL GAME - THE OLD SCHOOL

It is difficult to change anything, but allow me to explain my reasons for change. Young people coming into the game of soccer should not be subjected to a 'Horses For Courses' agenda. What is most disturbing is this idea that there is only the one game that counts, the second-ball game. Former professional players who now work for the media in England still hanker for the tackling game and some have even gone around the world pushing their second-ball game agenda. Most of the coaches come from the old school of thought and support the 'Forward-moving Game', one that is conveniently dumbed down for all kinds of reasons. The result of their comments on television is that most soccer supporters who watch week in and week out don't see the micro reality that exists within the game. What supporters see is based on what is the obvious direction and objective of play, which is to score goals at either end of the pitch. The fact that it is in effect an artificial way of playing soccer because forward is the only direction of play, is not known to the average supporter of the game. It is relatively easy to keep a lid on things nowadays. We have a closed shop media environment, where only the one truth exists. The rhetoric of the pundits supports the forward-moving game, without question. Anything other than their 'Forward-moving Mantra' would obviously question their belief system.

THE HORSES FOR COURSES AGENDA

In the forward-moving game, the development of the player does not require the coach to know a great deal about consequential physical movement forms or about how the body generates strength. The latter is especially true when the only game in town is based on the religious mantra of the 'Forward-moving Game'. Time stands still in many a soccer club, where 'Fitness training' and lots of forward running is all anyone is required to work on, which is then topped up by weight training that supports the big and strong mentality. Very few coaches would even think about controlling the training environment in such a way as to produce a certain physical development effect, one that can distinguish a physical being in a way that is specific to soccer. Many coaches who should know better prefer to ignore the reality, mostly because someone else creates the training program and expects that program to be implemented without question. They ignore the microcosm of the physical action moment during a soccer game. For example, when a player is in possession of the ball and is challenged, the obvious physical movement required does not entirely adhere to the forward-moving reality, but actually relates to movements that come from the lateral dimension. This is a problem for any coach that supports the second-ball game, so they simply ignore it. The resulting forward-moving mentality is mostly in place, which is enforced by those who sit firmly in the forward-moving world and believe in a type of game that in many ways is consequential to that reality. One of the obvious effects of the forward-moving mentality is the acceptance of hard challenges to win possession of the ball, which was and is still seen as the right way to go about it. In fact, when a player's mentality is encouraged to be forward-moving only, considering no other direction in play, this will certainly be backed by aggressive play. The second-ball game supporters and the pundits and the managers accept this and if injuries take place then they say "Oh well, it's a contact sport." The lack of truth hides the reality that many of the players who played the so-called beautiful game of the past and maybe even in the present expected to be clattered. Some even relished getting clobbered, which to my way of thinking is questionable from a psychological point of view. Some of the so-called old school players now obviously regret the effects of such an attitude, having to live with long term health problems that arose from hard tackles on the legs. Even now, Cup games still pander to the style of the "good old" days.

THE GOOD OLD DAYS

I wonder if the truth about the good old days does not go even much deeper than that. What lies beneath the surface of the hard tackling game? Why were the games often played on hard, muddy pitches on cold winter days, where being clattered was normal? Old traditions never go away. Just look at the time of year soccer is played in a country like England. Is it simply a coincidence that so many of the old school players are now suffering the consequences of the aggressive mentality? I think not. I believe this was and maybe even now is the case.

THE DIFFERENT FORMS OF PSYCHOLOGICAL CONDITIONING

I don't believe that advertising the brutal sport of boxing just after or before a game of soccer on television, for example, is an accident. Can watching boxing or loving the brutality of the hard tackle be related to the human condition and therefore one that requires gratification from violence? I believe it is! Sometimes I wonder about the psychology of anyone who relishes violence in sport, no matter what form it takes. Of course, almost all sporting endeavors carry some form of risk to the participant. However, such things should be accidental and not something that proves anyone to be a 'Man'. Winning possession of the ball in a game like soccer will always carry some physical risk, that is true, but the difference exists in the mentality and technical method of how this is done.

THE WORKING MENTALITY

When a manager imposes the forward-moving game on his players, he does not concern himself with or keep to any imaginative game plan. This can be seen in the following training session in support of the second-ball game, which simply mirrors the forward-moving game. In this case the coach keeps the training session based on what is known as the 'Drill' –

Note - The concept of the drill was supposed to represent repetition, but the word repetition in this case is somewhat misleading. A drill in the context of the forward-moving game is actually a game type practice, or the so-called shadow training concept. This is a practice pattern of play that supports only the forward direction of play.

THE FORWARD-MOVING DRILL

THE SECOND-BALL GAME

The movement pattern is set to a strict forward-moving objective – No pass backs here! The above may not look like much of a reference but is in fact very revealing. It's not about what you see, it's about what is not there. Shadow training consists of a starting position, which is always from a midfield player and not from the back of the defense, which in itself is revealing. The second-ball game does not implement the mentality of working the ball from the back of the defense, hence the starting point of the practice is from a midfield player, whose job it is to play the ball to the outside right, who then dribbles it down the line and crosses into the penalty area, where a striker is waiting to get in on the end of it and score. Crossing the ball into the penalty area is also called the percentage game, due to the belief that if the ball reaches the so-called danger zone, the striker has at least as good a chance as the defender to get his head on it.

THE ABSENTEE OUTSIDE LEFT

The above diagram shows the lack of lateral thinking in the game, even today. The lack of proper development of players ensures a lack of two footed capability, in which case it is not unusual to see that in many soccer clubs there are very few players proficient with the left foot. Once upon a time here in England, the National Team had a problem. They had only one left footed player to their name. The dominant forward-moving mentality resulted in absurd realities where in the whole of the country you could count the number of players with a left footed capability on one hand. The direction of this second-ball game practice session accounts for the lack of two-footedness or the lack of left-footedness in players. It simply concentrates on working the ball down the right side of the pitch, while use of the left side of the pitch is almost a token gesture. This is not an accident. It is convenient because the lack of left-footedness in the club, and therefore the lack of balance in the team (no natural left sided players), naturally lends itself to creating a game based on mistakes, simply because the practice session is skewed in favor of the right footed players. The left side of the pitch is mostly ignored and so when a right footed player is forced to play on the left side of the pitch, all sorts of problems emerge.

THE RIGHT-HANDED MENTALITY

When you consider what takes place in the social order, where the use of the right hand is dominant and the source of soccer players into the game is more likely to be based on the consequential one good foot, it is what it is. The domination of the game by the one-footedness reality is not that difficult to maintain. As far as the scouts were concerned, the lack of two-footedness or the lack of left-footedness in players is conveniently accepted and never questioned. That the player has only the one good foot to his name, which is the right foot in the majority of people, is OK because this actually caters to the "busy game" of soccer, where mistakes or a lack of ability is what is required.

MORE SUPPORT FOR THE SECOND-BALL GAME

It is also worth noting the psychology side of the above session, where everything had to be played forward. In this type of game, the midfield players are not creative but are defensive minded. This defensive mentality kills any notion of skillful play. The quality of the performance by the participants is not questioned nor are they encouraged to do anything special with the ball. Their job is to keep the game simple, adhering to the team shape and playing the ball wide to the right sided player. The outside right was simply encouraged to run forward with the ball and cross the ball into the opponent's penalty area, where again there is a designated striker (the number 9) whose job it is to try and head the ball into the back of the net. Nothing in this practice session relates to actual player development, regarding the player's ability to perform the details of the game, that can make the difference in the quality of performance.

COMPLEMENTARY METHODS

The practice of simulations mirroring the needs of the second-ball game was also backed by another idea, one that stopped development in its tracks, namely the conditioned game of soccer. This is where the players were only allowed two contacts with the ball. This type of conditioning is not about encouraging skillful play, but is designed to support the forward-moving game. The coaches never question the quality of the work or the one-footedness of the players. The lack of quality of the work is not questioned because this also has the desired effect of promoting lots of mistakes and creating the busy game, the second-ball game.

THE SOCIAL ATTITUDE TO THE GAME OF SOC-CER

In England, the forward-moving mentality was so entrenched that any notion of playing the ball to any other direction than forward would be met with a negative response.

THE LONG BALL FROM THE GK

The shout of "play the ball forward" came from the coaches, who feared losing. When the game was played by even younger players, coaches and the parents alike would shout similar instructions. Whether it's bad instructions or the way the game is expected to be played, everyone ignored the reality that simply hoofing the ball forward at every turn has nothing to with development. This way of playing is simply a second-ball game format and as such is of little value to the development of the individual. In the illustration above, we see what is in effect a functional game of soccer. The left back's position is the closest anyone gets to playing the ball out from the back of the defense. Even in the rare occasion that the goalkeeper throws the ball out to the left full back, that player in turn launches the ball forward down the line. To this very day this type of game is based on a culture that was cultivated and developed by those who benefited from the 'Second-Ball Game'. In any case, in such a culture the need to dumb the game down was obvious.

THE POSTAGE STAMP MENTALITY

How it works is rather simple. When the goalkeeper has the ball, every player from both sides takes his place in the middle of the pitch, in the so-called postage stamp position, awaiting the long kick. The keeper would then kick the long ball into this postage stamp line up (the 'postage stamp' was also called 'the mixer' or 'the battle ground'). Wherever the ball would land, players would fight for possession. Because such a ball coming down from upon high would cause problems, actually getting a hold of it would most likely fail on first contact, in which case both teams would have to fight for possession of the ball. If successful, this would be as a result of winning what is now referred to as the second ball. Even in a children's game, playing the long ball down the line was the only option. If a child hesitated, the shout from the man in charge and the baying parents on the sideline would soon put them right. The shout would be 'Get rid of it!', the meaning of which was to hoof the ball forward as far as you can.

NOT CREATIVE

As a result, the game in England became less skillful and did not begin from the back of the pitch. In fact, it is only in recent times that some teams have attempted to play the ball out from the back. But because this is a newer practice, playing the ball constructively from the back of the defense is still not a comfort zone for most players, especially the ones that come from the forward-moving mentality and the resulting limitation on skills that goes with it.

DEVELOPING MUSCLE MEMORY

The effect of this constant practice developing the muscle memory to a forward-moving mentality was never a question of whether the player can do more with the ball but always about the first habitual move that he will make. Remember that all forms of training have the effect of creating the bank of muscle memory relevant to the task at hand.

IN THE ABOVE DIAGRAM

When the players are encouraged to attack open spaces to the front of them, this enforces the first thought decision to run forward first and then pass the ball as a second option. In the above example, the player takes the ball up on the right foot and runs forward, regardless of any other game type option. How far the player will run with the ball is sometimes only dictated by the absence of opponents. It's not uncommon to see a player run forward with the ball at his feet for some fifty yards and only then think of what to do next. The second-ball game is reflective of the forward-moving priorities and not on any exchange or sharing possession of the ball. When the game is dominated by the forward-moving mentality, the lack of skills in players has been covered up by changes to the way the team defends, especially in their goal area. The manipulation of the players in the following team shape has them playing in designated zones, which is done to hide the lack of work with players on their skill level.

MARKING ZONES – THIS IS HOW THE GAME IS PLAYED

Surprisingly, such a way of thinking was not always the case. There was even a time back in the early seventies when Leeds United played the first-ball game. A lot of things changed when the powers that be introduced the 4–4–2 team shape. The manipulation of the players in this system has them playing in designated zones, which makes things simple. Why bother to create a game of soccer based on skillful play if the name of the game is stagnation because the club can't advance into the higher levels of the game. In modern times the game of soccer is much more defined for purpose. The back four in the 4-4-2 implements a zone defense which was introduced into the game because the worry was that the game was not exciting enough for the supporter. So, in order to make the game look good from a spectator point of view, some teams implement a zone defense for the sole purpose of making things easier when it comes to opening up the door for more goal scoring opportunities. It's exciting because this way of defending (zone positions with no cover) creates one on one situations, so a one-footed striker has some chance of breaching such a defense. In other words, a zone defense is a cover for the lack of skills in players. So why bother to coach and develop players with good attacking or defensive skills when you can solve the problem by killing two birds with one stone? Problem solved! The above solutions have nothing to do with development. It is a way of dumbing down the game and covering up for a lack of skills. The team shape makes it possible to designate functional roles and this enables the coaches to assign a given role to each player. How the game unfolds depends on the quality of the players and on whether there are restrictions placed on them.

CHAPTER FIVE

FURTHER MANIPULATIONS OF THE TEAM SHAPE

Very often it is the skill level of the players that determines how the game is played. All other options come under the heading of "Tactics". If the club is interested in commerce, they will try to play the game in a way that promotes the strikers. The 4–4–2 is an ideal platform for any number of solutions. One of them is making the strikers famous, because this sells shirts. To achieve fame and fortune for the striker, the rest of the players in the team work hard to pass the ball to him either inside of the penalty area or just to the outside of the penalty area. Should he receive the ball, he is the one licensed to score the goals. Getting the headlines is the name of the game. If a striker is good in the air, the team will try to get lots of crosses into the opponent's penalty area. Of course, this type of thinking is not about sharing goal scoring opportunities between all the players in the team, for that is a different game altogether. Promoting a striker's fame is driven by commercial interests and promoting a brand. Promoting the striker has the effect of promoting the image of the club, therefore the brand name. However, no matter what the excuse, this way of playing belongs to the second-ball game mentality. Quality players in their own right would have to swallow their pride, think of the money, should they have to play that way. In some ways, you can create a team that does the donkey work for the strikers and their opportunities to score the goals and get the headlines. There are teams in the English Premiership that do play in the name of commercial interests. Such teams usually languish in the middle of the league table.

CULTIVATING THE WRONG CULTURE

The English supporter is conditioned to believe in the existence of the "British game", a game of hard men and harder tackling. If the player on the ball is tackled hard from behind and left lying on the ground in a heap, it is seen as simply part of the British game. Yes, of course during the sixties the game was brutal, but not always. Certainly not in Sir Stanley's time. As far as I am concerned, the spectacular game of soccer should be based on creative play and not on kicking opponents when they are in possession of the ball.

BAD REFEREEING

If you can't match them for skills, cheat. In recent times the solution against a team that is skillful has been the use of the so-called 'Dark Arts'. Tapping ankles, tugging shirts, planting an elbow in the face, applying a knee to the underside of the spine, border line tackles, pulling shirts, spitting, goading, non-existent injury simulations etc. This way of playing is much easier than having to work hard and develop the correct solutions for the defensive or attacking side of the game. The dark arts have been sustained because nobody cares how the team plays, just as long as it wins. It is not that difficult to cover up for the lack of skills in players, especially when you practice the dark arts. Rather than coach, just take the easy way out and instruct the players to fall down as if struck by lightning or implement other tactics that have little to do with fair play. Make the players stay in their designated positions, apply 'The Horses For Courses' mentality, adhere to the forward-moving mindset, play the long ball game ... all of this has become foundational to the game of soccer in recent years and none of it has anything to do with development.

WHEN MONEY TALKS

All of the above manipulations of the game can be said to be professional in every way. However, the vested interests in the top clubs are not interested in traditional solutions. They are only interested in protecting their investment, which means paying for and creating the first team in the club based on the most skillful players money can buy. In the world of soccer today the spanner in the works can be said to be not in the hands of those who support the forward-moving game but in the hands of business. I am referring to the game now being dictated by the amount of money the owners of a soccer club are willing to spend on players. Clubs with deep pockets will always aspire to find the best players money can buy, from anywhere in the world. Naturally, an influx of more skillful players will affect the creation of a different game of soccer to that of the second-ball mentality. A skillful player is quite comfortable playing in a game where sharing possession of the ball is a normal experience, known as 'The Pass & Move game' or 'The first-ball game'. Some countries and quite a lot of top professional clubs now have no choice but to aspire to play with first-ball game mentality.

UNABLE TO COMPETE

There are hundreds of professional soccer clubs in the world, some with less money than others. The lack of progress for many of them is simply down to a lack of funds. The problem of how to keep going in their respective league, especially if the club is struggling to survive and has no immediate prospects of moving to a higher level, is to apply a 'Horses For Courses' team strategy. If a club plays in the lower divisions of the league, has no supporter base to speak of, and their survival is a matter of practical realities, there will be no interest in player development, only in keeping the playing standard of the team at a level that keeps the club where it is. Such a club does not depend on developing players in their own time, but will bring in players from outside, either discarded players, loan players or late comers into the game or even players that have retired from the top flight but are still able to play. The players coming in are vetted (compared) for their ability, or lack of it, which must be comparable with the needs of that club. However, once a player comes into such a club, on the horses for courses basis, it is rare for them to go back up again. If the player fits the status quo, then he comes in. There are ninety two (92) clubs in English soccer and the 'Horses For Courses' ideology can be found in every section of it, whether it's 'The Championship' or 'The Premiership'.

THE CONVENIENT WORKING SYSTEM

The Championship Clubs and the Premiership Clubs are complicit in supporting the second-ball game mentality. Why is that the case in this modern world? One reason is because the top clubs in the league bring in players and if they don't make the first team grade (many of them don't) they are either let go or given the opportunity to go out on loan to prove their worth. If it works, the club could call them back. If not, maybe the loan club will offer them a contract. But if that doesn't happen, then maybe the player could go down to the lower divisions, or worse, out of the game altogether. Such a way of doing business does not always work, so if the club makes mistakes in their procurement of players, the result can be a disaster in the form of relegation. None of this is related to any player development concerns. A player either makes it or is simply let go.

CHAPTER SIX

A CHANGE IN PSYCHOLOGY – THE FIRST TOUCH OPTIONS

The real game of soccer, which is the first-ball game, requires the development of the following foundational first touch options to the ball:

1 – MOVING THE BALL OFF THE LINE

2 – THE REVERSE TOUCH

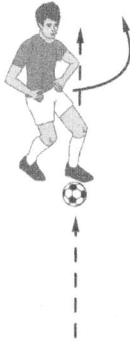

3 – THE EXTENDED FOOT TOUCH

4 – THE SET UP TOUCH

5 – THE ROLL TOUCH

6 – THE DINK TOUCH

7 THE FORWARD TOUCH

THE TWO-FOOTEDNESS CAPABILITY

Implementing the above first touches to the ball creates a multi-directional attitude to the game, which naturally changes the playing mentality and therefore the way the game is played. The extended foot to the ball touch, for example, affords the possibility of playing the ball to a wide range of angles. Every opportunity in the game of soccer begins with a first touch to the ball with purpose. The purpose could be to keep the ball or to pass the ball on. If the player keeps the ball off the first touch, he also needs related close ball control skills, such as drag backs for example. Having a good first touch to the ball and a repertoire of close ball control skills helps the player to construct effective first-ball game solutions. Such objectives can't be achieved by a conditioned game of soccer, certainly not in the name of player development.

KEEP OUT - IN THE NAME OF VESTED INTERESTS

In some quarters of the game, the prevailing horses for courses mentality is unfortunately deep rooted in the system and because of that, certain prevailing attitudes have become the norm, even if they are absurd, especially the ones where new innovations are seen as a threat to existing coaching practices. The 'Horses For Courses' criteria is upheld with a different psychology throughout the league, one that is not creative but is simply based on a forward-moving mentality where the game is reliant on the big and strong player. Where there is any development taking place, it is said to be specific to the club and based on the coach's philosophy. This is not player development territory! A second-ball game philosophy involves deliberate exclusion of skillful players in preference to the big and strong. The training method to develop a wide variety of skills simply does not exist, or is even understood. In the horses for courses mentality, where many skills are excluded in order to dumb down the game, the training methods deliberately exclude certain skills from the working repertoire. It's obvious that the prevailing psychology is based on the forward-moving mentality and so it's essential to omit any meaningful practice of certain skills. Certain skills require a lot of work because we are talking about developing the muscle memory to perform them. Let's talk about one such skill, the skill of moving the ball off the line. This is a seriously consequential skill which is deliberately left out of many a training session, through ignorance or deliberate action. The psychology of training is focused on skills that are forward-moving only and so not on any skill that would question the forward-moving mentality. Ignoring one of the most important factors of development is supported by creating specific habits, the kind of habits (the muscle memory bank) that are relevant to the type of game that is required. I am sure this is well known. The main reason that this particular skill is left on the sidelines is because this one touch option is not a forward-moving one and, if implemented, changes the playing mentality.

MOVING THE BALL OFF THE LINE REPRESENTS AN ENTIRELY DIFFERENT PLAYING MENTALITY.

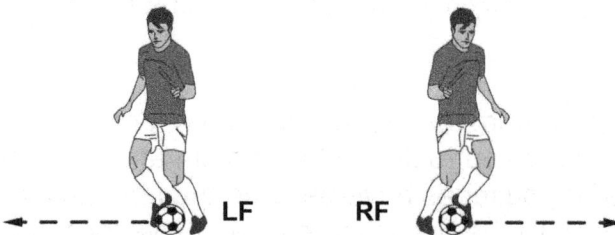

RF – The ball played with the inside instep of the right foot, this moves the ball to the lateral angle, to the left of the player.

LF – The ball played with the inside instep of the left foot, this moves the ball to the lateral angle, to the right of the player.

THE LACK OF TWO-FOOTEDNESS

It is no surprise that second-ball game coaches don't spend any significant time on this touch option. It is unfortunate but true that when it comes to development, conventional thinking also omits serious work on the development of two-footedness, which is consequential to the game of soccer. The lack of two-footedness is convenient because this too contributes to the lack of skills and is supportive of a second-ball game mentality. For those that support the second-ball game, what counts is keeping the players on the one good foot and forward-moving. Performing such a skill as moving the ball off the line creates not only a different playing mentality but also a different physical ability and, yes, a different way of working on or playing soccer.

EQUAL OPPORTUNITIES

There are many reasons why I have always advocated a different approach to the youth side of the game, especially when it comes to player development. Why should the development of children coming into the game be conditioned to emulate what goes on in the adult game? There should never be a 'Horses for Courses' interest in the development of young people and most certainly no deliberate manipulation of the type of skills learned. Most certainly, never discard any talented children to appease the big and strong criteria. It seems unbelievable, but children as young as ten years of age are chucked out of the game for no other reason than failing to appease the horses for courses criteria, which is absurd.

THE NAME OF THE GAME

Why do we call it a first-ball game? This name is just a way of describing the main feature of the game, which is keeping possession of the ball, but in a skillful manner. The level of skills must be much higher than in a second-ball game because the first-ball game is based on passes to feet and therefore on sharing possession of the ball. The first-ball game is not about promoting the one striker. It's about promoting the team. The game is dominated by short rather than long passes, which gives everyone the opportunity to contribute something constructive to the game. Another interpretation is that the first-ball game is a game that is multi-directional. In practical terms, any player in possession of the ball is supported from all angles and in this way the players create intricate movement patterns to any direction with the purpose of keeping possession of the ball and creating goal scoring opportunities. Everyone is equal in a first-ball game team. Because of this, such a team does not have designated strikers because when creating the movement patterns that enable the team to enter the opponent's defensive third, anyone in a favored position is licensed to finish the move off with a goal scoring (finish) opportunity. In the second-ball game the opportunity to score a goal is not based on sharing possession of the ball and can be restricted to certain players in the team, such as the designated strikers that we saw in the 4 – 4 – 2 line up.

REGARDING THE FIRST-BALL GAME TOUCHES TO THE BALL

THE CORRECT FOUNDATIONS

The most skillful players have a physique that is built on the fast twitch muscles. What everyone should take into account is the need for longevity in players. The big and strong second-ball game player is built around the slow twitch muscles, ones that require constant training to avoid putting on weight. If players are too heavy, they lose their speed and their ability to play effectively and often do not last long in the game. Players with a physique that is based on the fast twitch muscles through appropriate development formats from an early age have a longer shelf life and are therefore more capable for a much longer time span. The key issue in regards to the development of the player centers on the effect of any working solution. A special first touch to the ball option, one that makes the player most effective in the game, comes from the development of the fast twitch muscle forms. A coach, therefore, should know how to achieve the fast twitch muscle forms and what type of work the player should do in order to possess the physical ability to produce excellent soccer skills. How does the body function? What is the Anaerobic state of being? What is the Aerobic state of being? The answers to these questions give you the answer to what kind of development takes place in the muscles, what they are made of, and whether they are dominated by slow twitch or fast twitch muscles. It is possible to control the bias of the physical development of the player in favor of one or other forms of muscles. Promoting fast twitch muscles, for example, is one way of ensuring the development of the inner core strength, which is so essential to the quality of performance. It is therefore important to work on and develop fast twitch muscles if you want to develop skillful players. The big and strong players are made up of (predominantly) slow twitch muscles that can sustain a certain level of performance, but never as good as a player that is fast twitch orientated.

CHAPTER SEVEN

THE CORRECT PHYSICAL AND PSYCHOLOGICAL EFFECT

When you examine it in detail, you will find that the dominant feature of the first-ball game is to keep possession of the ball. It should therefore be obvious that keeping possession of the ball requires every player in the team to possess the ability to do so, therefore the player must possess the full repertoire of skills, especially as there are often times when the area of play leaves him with less than seconds to construct an effective solution.

NOT UNDERSTOOD

Fitness training for fitness's sake can be achieved by many means, and is likely to be more in tune with the second-ball game. The drill seen earlier can give the player a certain amount of work on his fitness, but that kind of fitness is second-ball game orientated. There is a separate type of fitness required to play the first-ball game, one that gives the player the energy to keep the ball skilfully and to sustain this type of energy throughout the ninety plus minutes of the game. It is not that difficult to run in straight lines, especially forward, but it is another thing altogether to work physically to keep possession of the ball in tight spaces. This next example shows how to develop this special kind of fitness. This is a kinetic tension solution for the development of core strength. A strong inner core is foundational to the quality of performance, with or without the ball. This work ensures the development of a much better physical balance and is the only way to improve the situation of a lack of two-footedness. This is also a neutral exercise, one without any bias for accepting the use of two-footedness, psychologically and technically speaking. To achieve the set objectives of skillful play, the work has to relate to that kind of game and so all working solutions have the ball at the players' feet and the development of the muscle memory is fast twitch orientated. It is based on short touches of the ball, with the additional option of applying the skill of moving the ball off the line in order to develop the ability to implement a change in direction at will or be able to use a combination of touches to the ball when required to do so in tight areas of play.

THE NINE CONE PLACEMENT SOLUTION

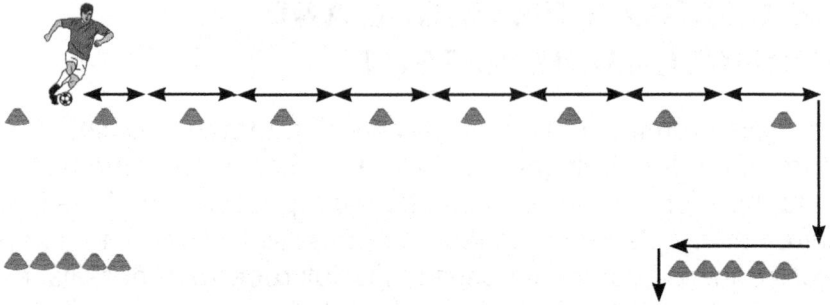

A FIRST-BALL GAME FORMAT

The first-ball game formats enable the player to move the ball to a working sequence relevant to a game of soccer that is based on keeping possession of the ball. All working formats touch the base of the Anaerobic state of being, which naturally brings the fast twitch muscles into the effort, which in turn develops a leaner and more effective physique. However, the energy spent returns more energy to the player in the long run because of a little thing called Entrophy.

NOTE - Most of the first-ball game formats are not slow twitch orientated, hence no long term problems of players becoming heavyset. Conventional training, on other hand, can have the long term effect of gaining weight, especially in the big and strong players.

FAST TWITCH ORIENTATIONS

The above working format is a worthwhile endeavor in the quest to also bring into the game a two-footedness capability which is foundational to the first-ball game skills repertoire. The work on the first-ball game continues apace, all of the time. It's not just for Christmas, as they say! In this Foundational Nine Cone Placement, Player A1 moves the ball sideways from gap to gap to the lateral angle, staying square on to the line of cones. The acceptance of using either foot to the ball develops the muscle memory necessary to use either foot to the ball from a physical and psychological point of view. This cone placement is also an introduction to the lateral dimension, which is important to the development of many first-ball game skills. This form of training counters the right foot leading problem in players that don't know any different by ensuring a different reality, a 'Two-footedness' leading capability. Another important aspect of this lateral based solution is to ensure the development of the correct balance between the right and left side of the physical body. The inside instep lateral movement objectives will ensure the correct muscle memory development on both the right and left side of the body, including the development of the collaboration in the brain between the left and right side of the brain, something akin to what takes place when someone is learning to play the piano. Many of the first-ball game objectives could never be achieved in any forward-moving one footed training environment. This is because, unlike the lateral format, the forward-moving environment only caters for the leading right foot, which in many ways is not as natural as you might think. For example, when it comes to finishing (striking a ball with the foot) many opportunities go begging because, if not trained up, the natural walking foot position gets in the way. In other words, the plantar foot position is so strong in its natural state that when the player attempts to strike the ball, he can't turn his foot to the laces of the boot position enough and so scuffs the ball with the inside instep of the boot. Following the work in the above format, we can be more specific when developing the correct plantar foot position of striking or passing the ball effectively.

THE PLANTAR FOOT POSITION

In this next example, which doubles as a ball possession practice session, the players work on the angle of the pass and on the shape of the foot position to the ball in relation to the chosen angle.

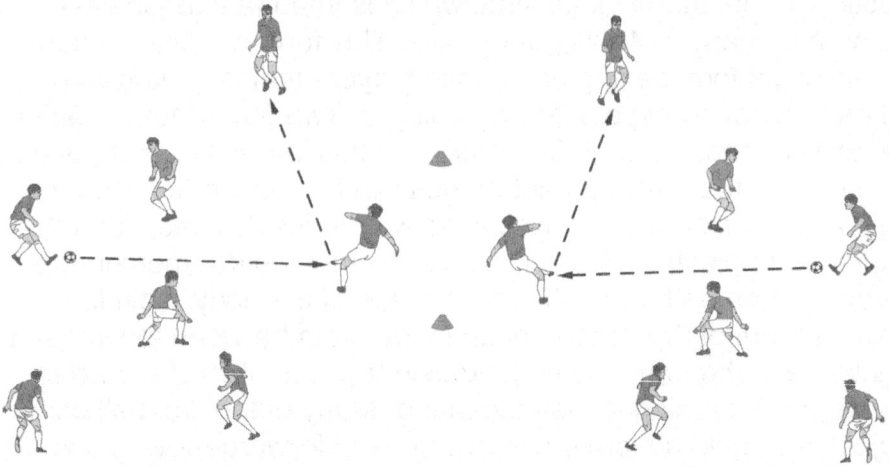

A KEEP THE BALL PRACTICE SESSION

On the right of the two cone placements, the player works the left foot inside instep to the ball, turning the left foot to the various angles possible to move the ball to the required angle, taking first the extended foot position touch and then using the same foot to pass the ball on to the next player. The opposite is true to the left side of the cone placements. All angled touches to the ball require the foot to be out-turned to the various angles possible. All first-ball game formats are rotational formats, which means every player takes his turn in the main theme of the practice format to keep the practice moving.

CONFIDENCE THROUGH THE ACQUISITION OF SKILLS

All working solutions should focus on developing the physical ability to acquire the first-ball game skills and if it is specific in that respect, this type of work can also change the mindset through the acquisition of a bank of memory of the soccer skills learned, which is a completely different reality to that of any second-ball game forward-moving mentality. The physical development from the 'Nine Cone Placement' to other forms lays down the foundations for a better skills level. The secret lies in working to the physiological principles known as kinetic tension. In other words, creating the right physical conditions that will employ the fast twitch muscles and promote and develop the strength in the inner core. A strong inner core forms the basis for developing the quality of technical performance which is necessary to perform many of the first-ball game skills consistently. A strong inner core gives the player the ability to pass the ball to any distance or to strike the ball with a quality of touch that makes the ball move through the air purposefully. Slow twitch muscle forms will not produce this kind of quality. Any coach worth his salt knows what I am talking about when I mention the quality of the strike or pass of the ball. Of course I keep banging the drum of the need to develop a two-footedness ability.

A SIGNIFICANT TEST OF ABILITY

It is not difficult to prove the value of such work. This next example enables the player to work on his balance and ball control. You can spot the underdevelopment of the player by the lack of quality in his work.

THE COMBINATION OF TOUCHES DEVELOPMENT FORMAT

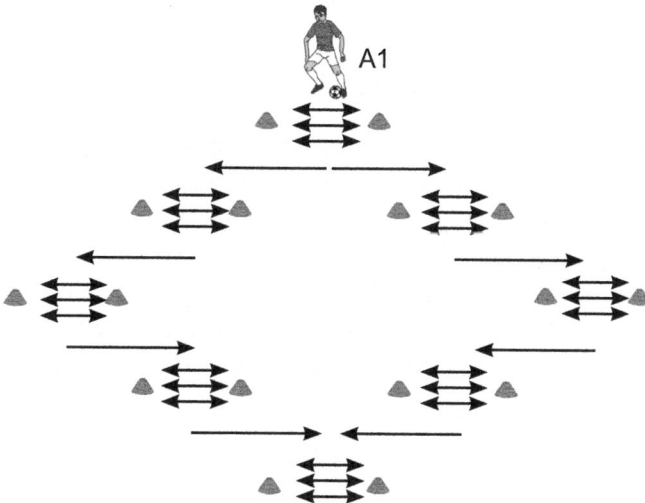

CONTROL THE LACK OF DEVELOPMENT

In normal game situations you will never spot the problems associated with a lack of ability in any individual player, especially if you watch a busy game of soccer. If you want to see whether a player is improving on both the physical and technical front, set this format up and let your players work with it and you will soon see what they are all about. If they can't do the work here then with certainty the player has his limitations. In this test the players have a simple task – Player A1 applies a sequence of short inside instep touches to the ball to move through the small gates. The inside instep touches are then immediately followed by moving the ball off the line. Next, the player takes a touch that should move him forward with the ball at his feet to the next gate. The short touches develop a feel for the ball and allow him to develop a comfortable attitude to working with the ball at his feet, to the left and right, without constantly looking down.

Note - The short touches to the ball with the inside instep of either foot through the small gates are lateral touches approximately 3 feet in length and the longer touch options are about 1.2 yards in length. Note the practice of combining short touches with the longer touch option of 'Moving the ball off the line' .

NO POINT IN AVOIDING SUCH A TEST

The truth is really simple. If the player is one-footed, he will not be able to move the ball to all the directions set by this format with any quality of touch. This means that the skill level is inadequate and so requires attention. If the player has developed a strong side to his body, it is logical to conclude that he will have a weak foot/side, in which case he will be out of balance and weaker on one side of the body. This creates obvious limitations. The lack of two-footedness creates habits that dictate the player's game which is clearly relevant to the playing standard.

CHAPTER EIGHT

MORE FORMS FOR DEVELOPMENT

THE PROGRESSIVE APPROACH

I started to create the first-ball game solutions back as far as 1992. At that time Barcelona was almost the only club on the continent of Europe that played the first-ball game. In those days, the great Johan Cruyff managed Barcelona, and his belief in the first-ball game brought the club great success. Barca has been the torch bearer of this style of soccer ever since. When Pep Guardiola, former Manager of Barcelona and Bayern Munich, made his way to the English Premiere League to take over at Manchester City, many doubted that he would be able to have success playing his trademark first-ball game style without great players like Messi, Iniesta, Xavi at Barca and Thiago, Ribery and Kroos at Bayern. It didn't take long for Guardiola and City to find success, winning the Premiere League in just his second season. I am glad that the world of soccer is at last catching up with the first-ball game ideology. More and more clubs in the English Premiership are taking to the first-ball game. Why? Because if they don't change their ways, Manchester City will keep on winning the titles, which means they will be left behind, with less money in their pockets. There are clubs in the English Premiership that are still the last bastions of the second-ball game. However, such clubs are struggling to stay in the Premiership. This is because some English Managers only know the second-ball game and have second-ball game players to work with. But it's not just in England where the second-ball game survives. Both Australia and America have been influenced by coaches that only know the second-ball game. I have mentioned why this is the case more often than not. Many managers only know the structured game of soccer. The first-ball game is not structured to any rigid team formation, as is the case when the players have designated roles and are discouraged from individual creativity or expression. The new generation of coaches in the game have a different mentality. The language of soccer is changing all the time. Clearly it is time to move forward, especially when it comes to the development of young players and their future in the game.

THE TRANSITIONS

Any transition requires the development of the switch-on moment to another phase of the game. This too requires training. I take care of this transition problem by implementing reaction training forms. There exist many transitions in the game of soccer, but the major ones are based on the transition of the team between the attacking phase and the defensive phase and vice versa. Whatever the phase of the game, every first-ball game player requires the implementation of relevant skills for any given moment. These have been worked out on the basis of educated observations directly related to the skillful game of soccer. Here are examples of how to develop the correct habits for the defensive phase of the game. The first-ball game applies the principles of defending based on 'Nearest Man to The Ball'. This was the case long before they tried to make the second-ball game look better by implementing a zone marking defense. The most effective first-ball game skills for the transition into the defensive phase are coached in a special way, from both the psychological and physical point of view. The players work on physical movements required to win back possession of the ball by legal means. In other words, by skillful means.

DEFENDING – REACTIVE ATTRIBUTES

The development of the thought process takes place in working formats that do exactly that, make the players think. There are many transitions of thought during a game of soccer. The following example shows how to connect with the transition of thought from one physical movement to the next. There is a theme to this exercise that also helps the players to develop concentration. The attacking players have a home base and the defensive players have a home base. The difference is they have an additional set of cones next to their planted sticks in the ground. The attacking side have a red cone base, the defensive side have a blue cone base. The blue and the red cones are placed on the ground next to the stick.

A TRANSITION OF THOUGHT FORMAT

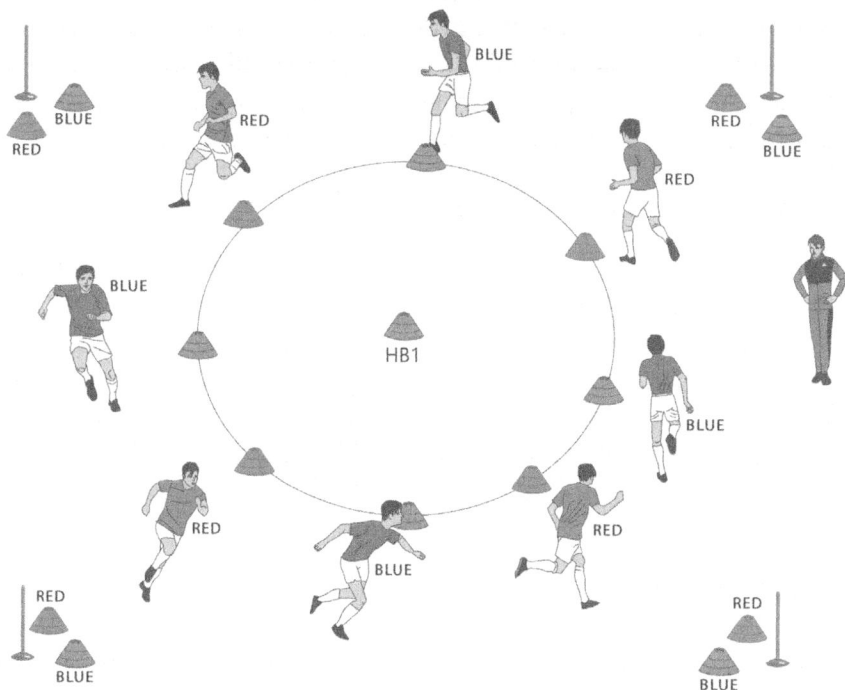

The attacking players have a home base and the defensive players have a home base. Each player starts in his cone placement and each position is said to be the player's home base. The attacking players have a blue cone base – the defensive players have a red cone base. This is the starting position for each player.

INSTRUCTIONS

Players work to either the clockwise direction or the anti clockwise direction. The coach shouts instructions. All players react – for example jog from one cone placement to the next – then walk one – players respond by going from one cone placement to the next performing the task requested by the coach – jog one walk one is repeated until the coach changes his instructions – players listen for the next call option – if the call is 'home base 1! Players sprint to the center circle and back to their original home base and stop. Listen to next call/instruction – protect your home base – on this call – there are four stations to the outside of the circle, each with a blue and a red cone at the base. The defensive players must place the red cone into the blue stick base before the attacking players move to any station and place their blue cone into place (the cones have a hole in the middle and they can slot the cone over the top of the stick and onto the ground) – instructions for the work around the circle could involve other calls such as – sprint 2 (sprint past two cone placements) – sprint to home base – all players sprint clockwise until they reach their home base.

DURING A GAME OF SOCCER

There are lots of physical movement changes taking place during a game of soccer. One minute the player is running, the next he is walking and the next he could be challenging for possession of the ball, receiving the ball, passing the ball, etc. We can improve the thought process with this type of exercise. The timing of instructions to the players should be such that the players must think quickly on their feet, which is the main objective of this format.

TRANSITION

All such examples deal with the development of the transition moment, which is something we can work on with reaction training formats. The development of fast thinking and the consequential fast physical reaction time can be developed with specific cone placement formats.

Transition training is just one part of the working equation, but probably one of the most important abilities any player can possess. A fast thinking brain also needs fast legs, and that too requires training. Such formats not only develop a fast thinking brain but when the player tries to perform the set task this has the effect of also developing the fast twitch muscles, ones that implement a fast reaction to any given problem in the game. Keep in mind that when in the defensive phase, this usually involves having to deal with a fast moving one-on-one situation because of the working principle known as 'Nearest Man To The Ball'. The art of defending has to first deal with the player in possession of the ball in terms of defensive priorities and the players that support the player in possession of the ball. Winning back possession of the ball is not based on marking zones as such. Zones don't score goals, opponents do!

THE PHYSICAL DEVELOPMENT FIT FOR PURPOSE

In this next section I am going to present the type of physical movements that players need to work on that will help them to make the correct approach to the player in possession of the ball and to have the fast feet ability to either mirror the movements of the player in possession or make the correct physical challenge for possession.

TAKING CONTROL OF SPACE AND TIME

"Never dive in" is a principle of defending worth remembering. We can sometimes see players being caught on the wrong side of the player in possession of the ball because they have been sucked in by a clever move. Staying goal side is always best in one-on-one situations. Closing the attacking player down is essential because there is no way of stopping a player from getting his pass away or a shot on goal by standing back. Closing down the opponent's playing options requires fast feet and good movement coordination. The nearest defender has to move forward quickly to the player in possession while always checking the run up to the lateral side – right or left of the opponent. This way of approaching the player in possession of the ball can make that player drop his head and look at the ball. This then could be the time to move quickly to the ball.

DEVELOP FASTER FEET

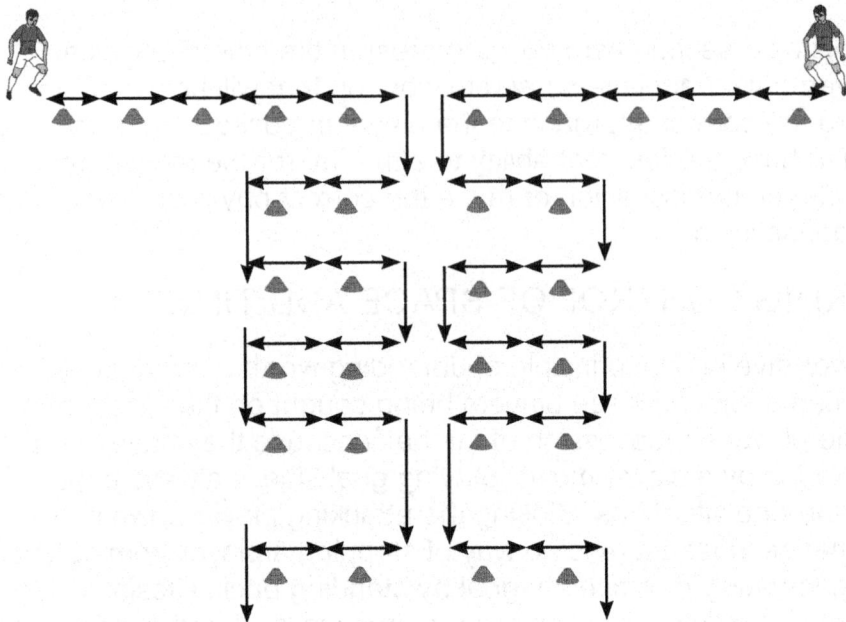

WORKING ON THE RUN UP

The nearest defender moves forward to the player in possession by checking the run up to the lateral side – right or left of the opponent.

THE LONGER RUN UP FORMAT –

In this next example – The 3x 10 yards run up – Here, the players work on developing the sideways (from a square on physical position) check out movements off of a forward run up. In competition mode, be first to complete the task.

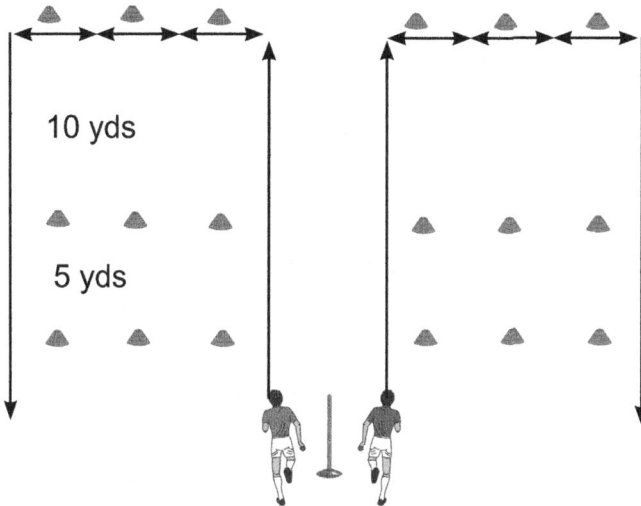

10 yds

5 yds

CHECK THE RUN UP - A COMPETITIVE FORMAT

THE NEAREST MAN TO THE BALL

The first challenger needs to get close, roughly 3 yards from the player in possession of the ball, if he wants to have any influence on the intentions of the attacking player. Showing the attacking player either to the outside line(to the right of the defensive posture) or the inside line (to the left of the defensive posture) depends on checking out your run up to ensure that defensive objective. This objective is achieved by having the physical ability to change the movement from forward to lateral and then even to the diagonal angle, left or right of the initial defensive approach. The run up to the attacker can be any length, usually around 10 yds.

THE JOCKEYING FORMATS

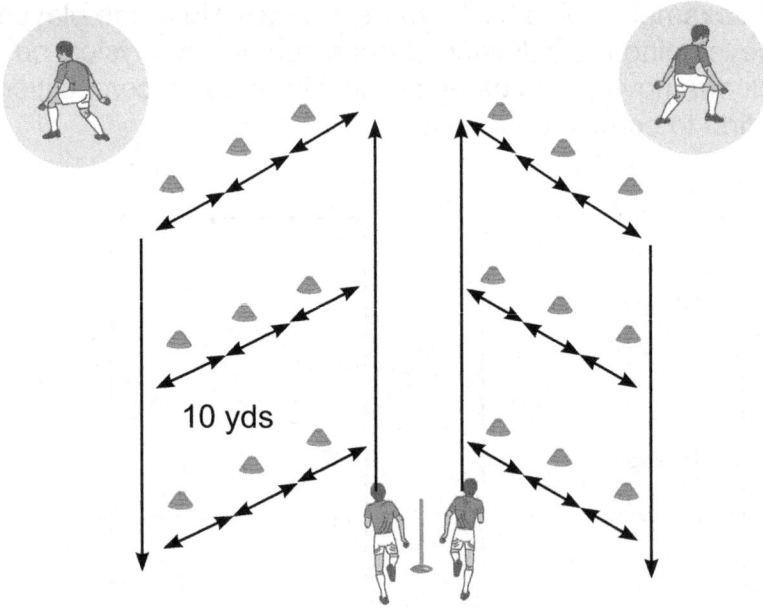

10 yds

THE COMBINED DEFENSIVE MOVEMENTS

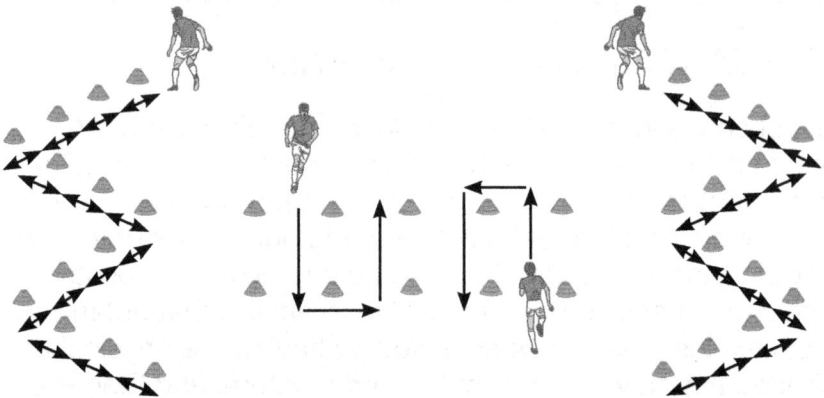

When the attacking player is very close to the defender, the defender has to have fast feet and the ability to move to any direction, not just the forward-moving direction. The practice here is all about moving the feet quickly over a very short distance, to the forward, lateral and backwards jockeying directions.

THE PRACTICE FORMAT PRIORITY OBJECTIVES

THE FIRST OBJECTIVE - Control the direction of play by keeping the opponents away from the direct line of attack.

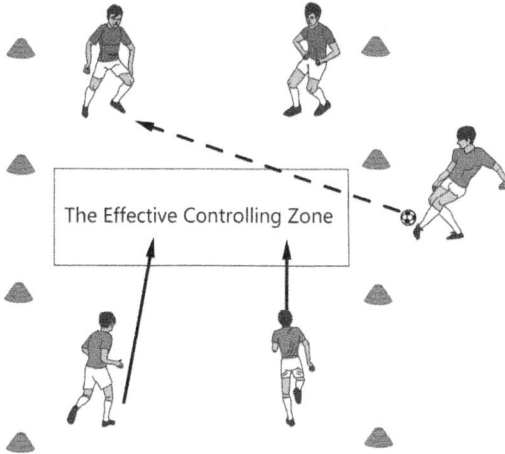

The Effective Controlling Zone

THE ART OF DEFENDING BASED ON THE NEAREST MAN TO THE BALL

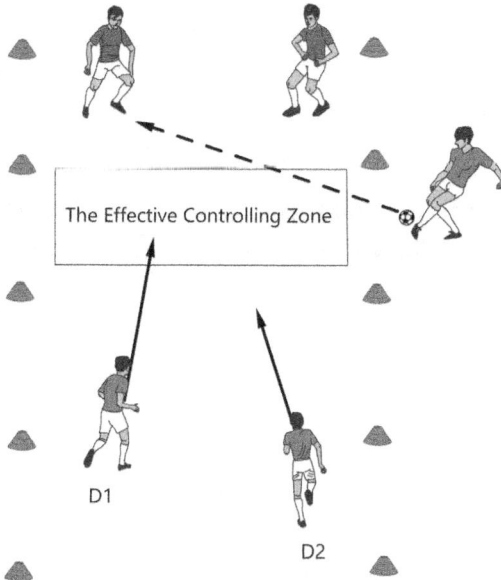

The Effective Controlling Zone

D1

D2

PRACTICE SENDING THE NEAREST MAN TO THE BALL

FOR D1 - practice moving up to the check out zone to place a bias on the options of player A2 and work on sending the player in possession to either the right or left.

The signal for the run up can be the pass from player SP1.

PRACTICE GIVING COVER TO THE FIRST CHALLENGER

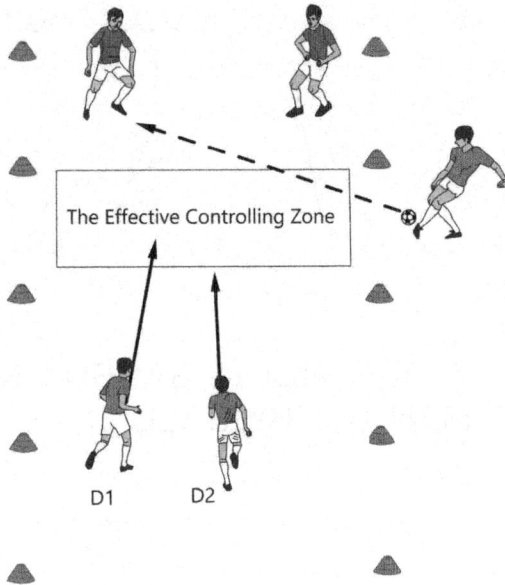

The Effective Controlling Zone

D1   D2

Player D1 is the first challenger, followed by player D2. This method affords a secondary challenge option by giving cover to D1.

THE ULTIMATE OBJECTIVE

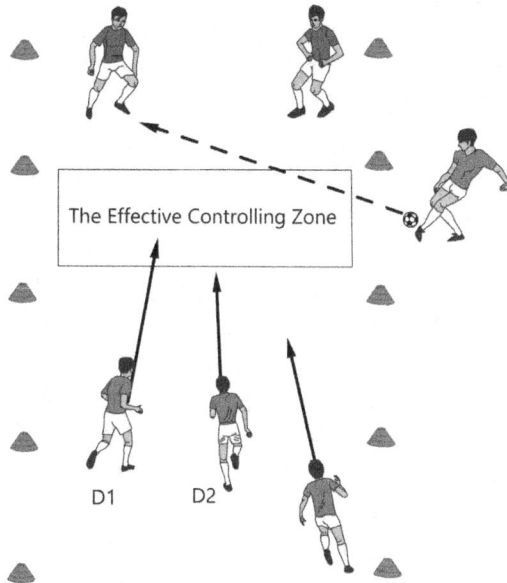

The Effective Controlling Zone

D1   D2

Move – On the pass from the service player, present the first challenger to the ball. Give cover for the first challenger and add more players to the defense who have the responsibility to take care of other opponents and their intentions that are obvious options to the player in possession of the ball.

WITHIN THE ABOVE EXAMPLES

When a first-ball game breaks down for whatever reason, there are plenty of players in the vicinity of the ball, mostly because the first-ball game team keeps the ball though a sequence of short passes. If the players are quick thinking, they can usually hunt the ball down with numbers and win the ball back. Obviously, everything happens quickly in a game and things can change in an instant. The above working formats relate to the 'Nearest Man To The Ball' principle and so what you see in overall terms should be enacted at the point of trying to win the ball back for the team, in which case all of the above working solutions are a representation of the micro world of the first challenger and the kind of physical skills that come into play even away from the actual challenge for the ball. The duties outside of the challenging area are just as vital to the defense. Winning possession of the ball involves employing a covering player behind the first challenger and even a third man who looks after the immediate zone behind both players to make sure there is no easy outlet for the player in possession. In some ways, knowing how the first-ball game is played makes it possible to know how to defend it. However, if the first-ball game team has very skillful players, that is easier said than done. It is hard to defend against a first-ball game team because a strict team defensive structure does not work against a free flowing team. Neither does applying a man-to-man marking system. The best way to defend against any team is to employ a structure in defense while having a nearest man to the ball policy. When you win the ball back, make sure you defend by keeping possession. The first-ball game is based on keeping possession of the ball, which once again means playing the short pass to feet, rather than hitting the long ball. This allows players to be in close support to the player in possession of the ball. So there is no true structure to that way of playing, most certainly not in the immediate vicinity of the ball, but a free flowing movement form that keeps possession of the ball, away from the opponent's reach. Such an objective is worked to any direction that achieves the set objectives of creating a goal scoring opportunity.

CHAPTER NINE

THE TRANSITION TO THE ATTACKING PHASE

When you bake a cake, you don't leave out half of the ingredients! One thing is certain, the first-ball game will always be down to the ability of the player to either create a goal scoring opportunity or to stop the opponents from creating a goal scoring opportunity. In either event it will always be a matter of development. The nine-cone placement is a lateral foundational format that affects all the phases of the game. However, when it comes to the first-ball game, the most important result of that development includes the laying down of the foundations for the development of the first touch options.

IT'S NOT A MATTER OF OPINION!

One way to hide the lack of development in players and what kind of game is played is to say that everything about the game is based on an 'Opinion'. Higher standards of play in any sporting endeavor, including the game of soccer, are most certainly not about opinions. Proper development is always down to hard work with the appropriate coaching solutions. The result of opinion is simple, the cake tastes horrible and it is half baked. There are lots of missing ingredients from the players' point of view. Take the art of passing the ball. I have never seen anyone work on the pass in training, always leaving it to the actual game. It's as if they be-lieve that's all that was required to become an excellent passer. In truth, passing should always be worked on in a meaningful way.

DEVELOP THE UNSELFISH MENTALITY

THE PASS 'OFF' THE OFF THE LINE TOUCH

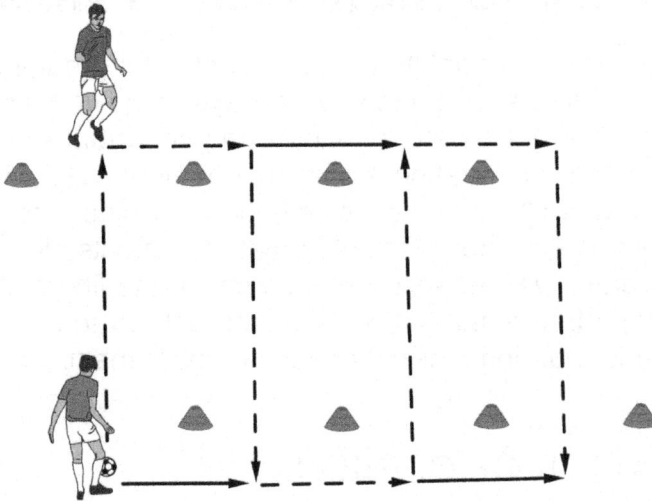

The first-ball game is based on sharing possession of the ball. It is simply the foundation of this type of game. Every player in the team plays for the team, not for selfish reasons. The habit of keeping the ball to make sure the player looks good on camera is certainly not the attitude required. The last thing a fast flowing game of soccer requires is players who don't have the ability to move the ball on quickly. What is required is the physical ability as well as the habit of having the right attitude to create effective solutions.

THE WORKING SEQUENCE

The ultimate objective of the pass and move sequence is to string at least five passes together. The inside instep work has its implications to all the skills of the game, especially when we are talking about the ability to play the ball off the line, so the emphasis here is on the off the line touch. You may also appreciate that the inside instep short lateral touches form the basics of this pass and move game.

NEXT EXAMPLE

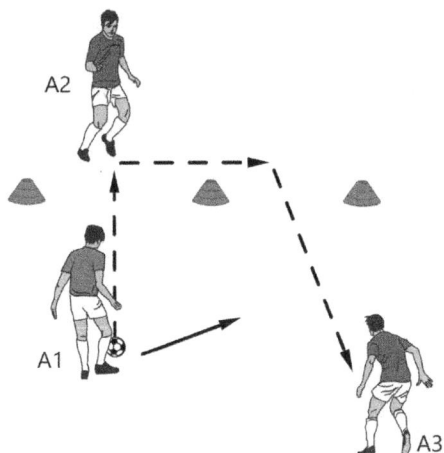

The development of the lateral ability, which is demonstrated by the inside instep work with the ball across the line of cone placements, is essential to many skills of soccer.

Note - if the player didn't have the lateral strength in his physical being, he would not be able to work the ball effectively. Moving the ball off the line to any direction requires lateral strength and the ability to use both feet. The practice requires the player to work to the right and left of the format.

Use a third man option format

The third man option – player A2 passes to player A1. Player A1 moves the ball off the line and plays the pass to the third man, player a3. Player A3 knocks the ball back to player A2. Repeat the working sequence moving down the line.

NEXT EXAMPLE

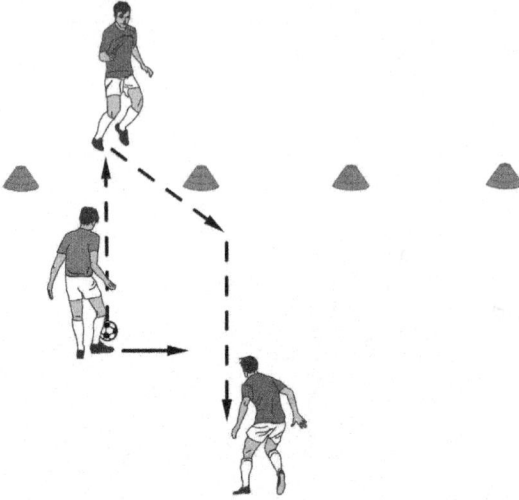

WITHIN THE SAME FORMAT

Taking the set-up touch to the ball (playing the ball with the inside instep to achieve the angle required to make the pass) is obvious, but what is not obvious are other significant issues, such as the timing of the pass, looking up, weight distribution, etc.

Touch the ball to this angle and pass the ball to the third man. The right foot set up touch – work to both directions - in which case the left foot would set the ball up for the right foot pass back.

Developing first-ball game habits - players cooperate with each other to work on the touches and pass option.

Changing the angle for the pass (a) setting the ball up for a long pass option (b)

Here we can see the practical application of the skills shown. The above are right foot examples but i would expect the player to be able to do exactly this type of work with his left foot just as well.

NEXT EXAMPLE

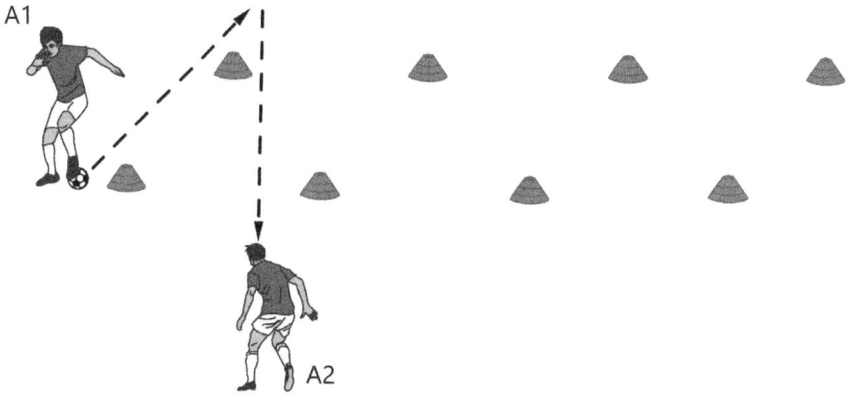

Practice pulling the ball back – player A1 pulls the ball back from the defender and this opens up the angle for the pass to player A2.

CHAPTER TEN

THE ANGLES ON THE FIELD OF PLAY

The following observations affect every playing philosophy. However, it is ironic that in so many ways, the first-ball game is not overly concerned with the angles that relate to the design of the soccer pitch. This is because in the attacking phase they are not expected to play in a structured game. They can take up and move to any position they wish.

THE LACK OF TWO-FOOTEDNESS IN GOAL SCORING OPPORTUNITIES

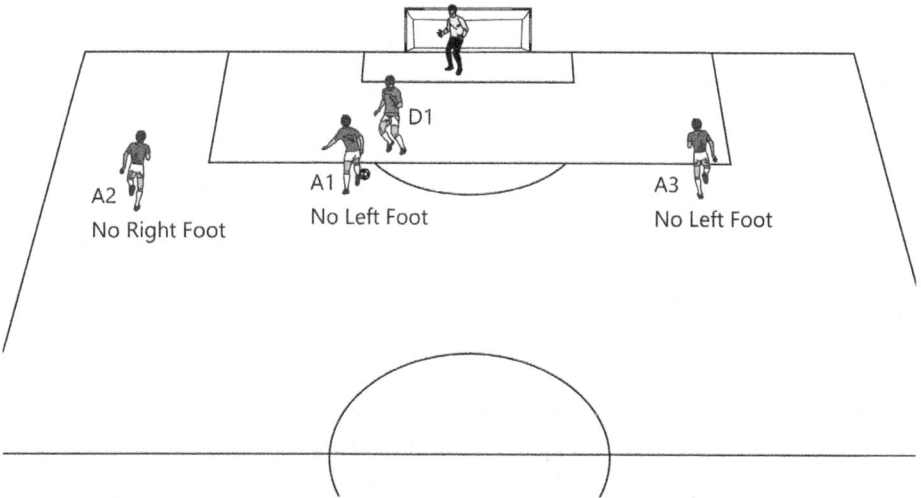

D1

A2
No Right Foot

A1
No Left Foot

A3
No Left Foot

IN THE ATTACKING PHASE OF THE GAME

This is not to say that the lack of two-footedness in relation to the angles on the pitch is not a problem. It is! However, the lack of two-footedness together with a strictly structured forward-moving game of soccer will affect the second-ball game player more, especially where the players have to stay in their respective zones.

NO LEFT FOOT – NO RIGHT FOOT

The angles on the soccer pitch should be factored into any worthwhile training session. How many times during a supposedly high standard game of soccer do we observe a right footed player moving into the left side of the penalty area and fail to score because he hasn't got a left foot to his name. I am talking about players that earn a lot of money from the game, but fail to deliver on expectations because of a lack of two-footedness or the appreciation of the angles related to the game of soccer. In the above example we have such a scenario, in fact it is not exceptional but quite a normal occurrence. The one-footedness of the attacking player A1 makes the job of the defender D1 easy. The defender only needs to ensure a block on the attacking player's right foot. I am sure that many coaches think this is pathetic to say the least, but nothing is done about it because it is the way it is.

ADAPTING THE WRONG WAY

IN THE STRUCTURED MENTALITY

The same applies to the idea of playing players in areas of the pitch that make them play out of their comfort zones. For example, a left footed player playing on the right side of the pitch or a right footed player playing on the left side of the pitch. All such ideas relinquish the responsibility for the proper approach to player development. The lack of two-footedness for no good reason is shored up by this nonsense. Why is it acceptable for players making millions to ply their trade with only the one good foot to their name? Why does nobody question the missed opportunities in front of goal because of the limitations of this one-footedness? Any coach who simply accepts this as an unfortunate reality and does nothing to try to develop more well balanced players is frankly not acting in the best interests of his players or his team.

A RELEVANT CONSIDERATION

The field of play from a practical point of view is divided up into four sections. Each section can be said to be a 90° surface area on the field of play. When the players are not in compliance with this reality and are only developed to be one footed, they will always find their relationship with the field of play compromised, especially so if the players play in a structured game of soccer and have their specific area to work in and are not allowed to venture beyond their allocated position in the team structure.

IN THE ATTACKING PHASE

MAKING THE CORRECT DECISION

PLAYER A1 SEEING LESS

Take this game scenario. In this example Player A1 has the ball at his feet. What will influence the choice of action for player A1?

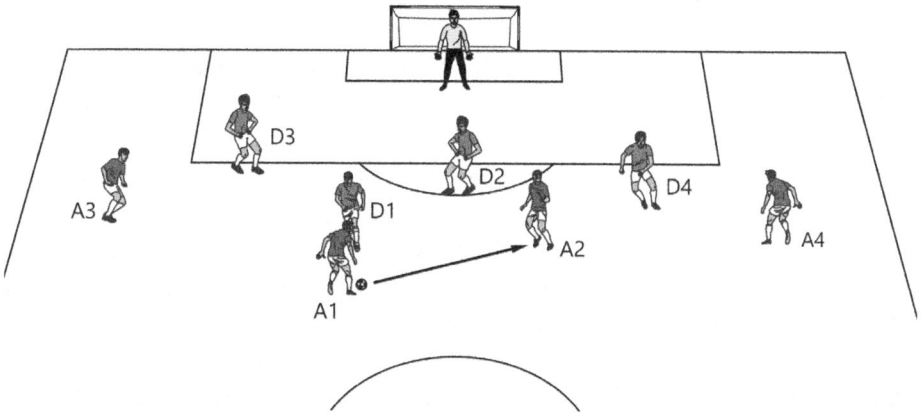

THE CROSS SECTION OF A SOCCER PITCH

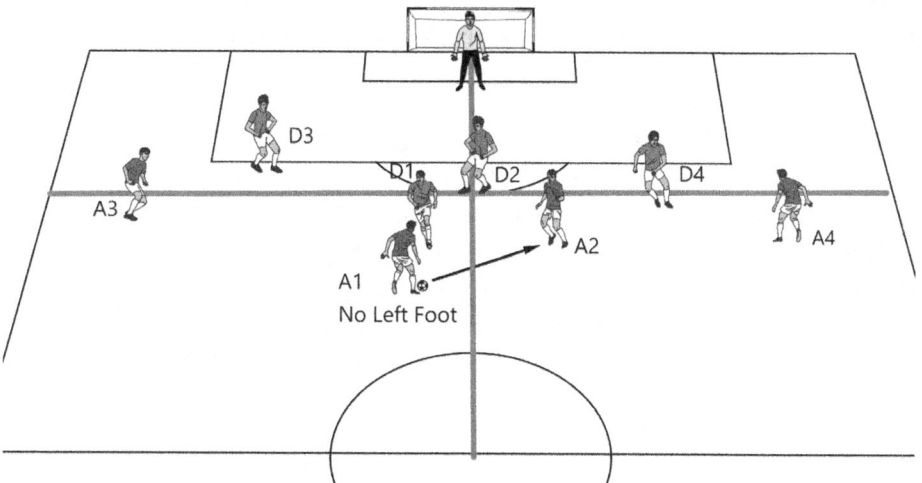

THE PLAYING ANGLE

In the above situation, when the player is confronted by the defender D1, the one-footedness of A1 will always result in his habitual use of his strong side to keep the ball. He will bring the ball to his right side and not see the whole picture in front of him, narrowing his playing options to just the 90° angle. Seeing less leads to mistakes, which is fine for a second-ball game mentality where creating the busy game through mistakes is what is required.

If the player is two-footed, on other hand, he has the opportunity to be more in control and his options open up to the full 180°.

THE DESIGN OF A SOCCER PITCH

Whether it is in England or in America or anywhere else for that matter, the design of a soccer pitch is a serious issue. Ignoring such issues and leaving them out of any development consideration can be said to be a second-ball game attitude. Ignoring the obvious design of a soccer pitch seems to be a preoccupation of those who fail to comprehend that in fact the game is played on a soccer pitch, which can be divided up into three major sections: The Defense Area – The Midfield Area - The Attacking Third. Such a division does influence events. This simple truth means little to those who stick to the forward-moving mentality and use drills or small sided games to work with players, as if any of the above does not matter.

NOTE;- I do not use drills – I use specifically designed formats that are detailed references for the skills that make up the first-ball game.

To continue - The field of play is not going to change anytime soon and that is the reason that this reality has to be factored into any youth development program. One thing is certain, when they support a second-ball game mentality, they don't ignore the area of the game known as the defensive third. In that area of the pitch playing the ball out of the defense by keeping possession of the ball is not a comfort zone for any second-ball game player.

NOT JUST TO THE 90°

There are some 720° of angles on the field of play related to the game of soccer, but only exceptional players can ever hope to play the game of soccer to at least the 360° possibilities. The most common standard of play in the world of soccer is based on the 90° angle, especially if the players are right footed and play in a structured team shape.

IN RELATION TO THE FIRST-BALL GAME

The first-ball game is getting traction in Europe. However, it is only players like the great maestro Messi who come close to using the 360° angle possibility. The existence of the second-ball game mentality prevents anyone from achieving the standard represented by players of this stature.

FROM A DEVELOPMENT POINT OF VIEW

Lionel Messi was lucky, he did not have to conform to the for-ward-moving mentality. The proper development of any player coming into the game should get him away from the forward-mov-ing mentality and help him recognize that the game is moving on and is made up of many parts, the most important of which is based on a proper first touch and a proper repertoire of skills that enable him to deal with challenges for possession of the ball. Keeping possession of the ball requires a higher energy and a higher level of skill. If a coach wants to improve players, there should never be a blanket solution because the field of play dic-tates what kind of skills apply or even how to play the game in those areas. Many coaches who support the second-ball game are quick to sing the praises of players like Messi, completely ignoring the fact that Messi is the player he is because he wasn't brought up with a second-ball game mentality. He was lucky enough to spend his developmental years in an environment which cultivated individual skill and creative freedom rather than the structured, stifling reality of youth football in England, America and other countries beholden to the second-ball game. Some of these coaches hold Certifications that fail conveniently to recog-nize the need to develop the type of skills that enable the player to play soccer within his own personal bubble and to play with a freedom that is not restricted by a structured team shape. Lionel Messi learned the difference between the skills he uses in his personal playing bubble and the skills he uses outside of that bubble, precisely because he was not restricted by any artificial means, such as conditioning players to two contacts. Such restrictive conditions hide the lack of skills by selecting players based on their strength, so a player like Messi would have been dumped out of the game long ago. Thankfully though, Messi did not end up in a country like England or America or in most European countries that follow the second-ball game mentality.

THERE IS A DIFFERENCE

If it was down to the second-ball game Managers, we would have never seen Messi on any soccer pitch. Thanks to the real freedom he experienced, Messi knows the difference, he knows what a second-ball game is all about, hence his success against any zone marking defense, which was and still is always more than obvious.

WHAT IS THE TRUTH?

The truth is that there is no such thing as a blanket solution to anything, certainly not when it comes to the first-ball game. For example, the art of taking a first touch to the ball should never be confused with any one on one skill. There are different skill requirements in every area of the field of play. Consider what happens in Zone D. During a first-ball game the defense plays the ball out from the back with a series of accurate passes because that is the safe option for them. Only in extreme danger does any player launch the ball out of this area. In the second-ball game, the defense behaves completely differently. They don't pass their way out from the back, but simply launch the ball as far from the defensive third as is humanly possible.

IN ZONE M

Have you ever wondered why a first-ball game team like Barcelona keep the ball better than most in the midfield zone? The answer to that is that a first-ball game team player knows the different ways of playing in the zones mentioned and so does not have a one size fits all mentality. When the players have a first-ball game skills repertoire and therefore more room in the midfield to work with (especially when the opponents drop back to park the bus in their defensive third) they keep the ball in this zone by keeping things simple and using the range of first touch options to the ball. In this way they create the movements that bring them into zone A where a different reality takes place. The first team players know what to do in the defensive area of the pitch and in the midfield area of the pitch. In teams where the skills are limited to the forward-moving mentality, players are designated to their functional roles. The team is spread all over the pitch and play as if every part of pitch is the same. There are no requirements to employ a different set of skills for any particular area of the game.

CRACKING A ZONE DEFENSE

When the skill level is defined by physical rather than skillful strength, the attacking side of the game is left to runners and solutions such as crosses into the opponent's penalty area. Runners and crosses of the ball into the opponent's penalty area give them the comfort of the busy game of soccer.

A DIFFERENT MENTALITY

What does the first-ball game team know about the attacking phase of the game when it comes to the attacking third of the pitch (Area A)? When the first-ball game team has advanced into the attacking third of the pitch, their ability to keep possession of the ball is key to any goal scoring opportunity. A first-ball game team does not rely on crosses into the penalty area, but uses controlled passes together with creative movement off the ball to create goal scoring opportunities. That is the difference! The development of the first-ball game player takes everything into account. The first-ball game requires a high level of skills. The development of any player, particularly one who aspires to play in attack, is all about developing the ability to take a proper first touch to the ball, which is complemented with other skills that enable the player to take on any defensive position. There is no blanket solution to everything because there is a difference be-tween one-on-one skills and the first touch options. The work on player development has to be specific to the needs of the game first and foremost and if it's the first-ball game then the skills must be relevant to that kind of game.

THE FUNCTIONAL GAME OF SOCCER

When it comes to the second-ball game, there is a blanket solution in place for everything, mainly because the second-ball game is based on functional roles and this type of game suits the horses for courses mentality. Keeping to functional roles creates a simplistic approach which lends itself to a system of training known as 'The Understudy of the Functional Role' (the designated team position for each player). The understudy method is an effective way of training up players for the functional role. In a typical second-ball game, every player adheres to his functional reality. For example, the full-back will be expected to keep things simple, which means that in fulfilling the functional role, he will be expected to play the ball forward and long at every opportunity. Using the long ball game is easy to keep under wraps. If two opposing sides are functional and therefore second-ball game orientated, the game will not be based on keeping possession of the ball and as a result neither of the teams will be in full control of the game. In other words, playing the long ball creates lots of transition moments and therefore a busy game of soccer, which is fine for those that deliberately dumb the game down and could not care less about how the game is played. The following statistics describe the reality of a second-ball game and its consequences. This take on the second-ball game is based on a true analysis of what actually takes place. The first point of observation needs to focus on what that team is doing when they are in possession of the ball in the most important area of the game, which is their defensive third. You will see that a second-ball game team lacks the skills to keep the ball in this area, so they simply play the long ball game.

THE MINUTE BY MINUTE REPORT

A SECOND-BALL GAME MENTALITY

From The Kick Off

GOALKEEPER	DEFENDERS
	9 seconds - Long Ball
	3 min 9 sec - Long Ball
	3 min 21 sec - Long Ball
4 min 24 sec - Long Ball	
	5 min 30 sec - Long Ball
	5 min 48 sec - Long Ball
	7 min 10 sec - Corner - Long Ball
	8 min 7 sec - Free Kick - Long Ball
	9 min 16 sec - Long Ball
	9 min 44 sec - Long Shot on Goal - No Goal
10 min 7 sec - Long Ball	
11 min 34 sec - Long Ball	
	12 min 19 sec - Long Ball
	12 min 57 sec - Long Ball
	13 min 43 sec - Long Ball
14 min 46 sec - Long Ball	
	15 min 10 sec - Long Ball
	16 min - Long Ball
18 min 30 sec - Long Ball	
	18 min 50 sec - Injury to player - time out
	19 min 42 sec - Long Ball
	20 min 9 sec - Long Ball
	20 min 39 sec - Long Ball
	20 min 55 sec - Long Ball
	21 min 51 sec - Free kick - Long Ball
	22 min 7 sec - Long Ball

GOALKEEPER	DEFENDERS
	22 min 40 sec - Corner - Long Ball
	24 min 20 sec - Long Ball
24 min 30 sec - Long Ball	
	25 min 29 sec - Long Ball
26 min 39 sec - Long Ball	
	27 min 48 sec - Long Ball
	28 min 17 sec - Long Ball
	28 min 31 sec - Long Ball
	28 min 53 sec - Long Ball
	29 min - Injury - Free Kick - Long Ball
30 min 11 sec - Long Ball	
30 min 35 sec - Long Ball	
31 min 9 sec - Long Ball	
	31 min 24 sec - Long Ball
	31 min 46 sec - Corner - Long Ball
32 min 16 sec - Long Ball	
32 min 43 sec - Long Ball	
32 min 57 sec - Long Ball	
33 min 13 sec - Long Ball	
	34 min - Header out - Long Ball
	34 min 35 sec - Free Kick - Long Ball
	35 min 10 sec - Long Ball - Cross into the Box
35 min 35 sec - Long Ball	
	36 min 5 sec - Injury - Time Out
	36 min 25 sec - Free Kick - Long Ball
	36 min 45 sec - Long Ball
	37 min 31 sec - Free Kick Short/ Long Ball Clearance
	38 min - Long Ball

GOALKEEPER	DEFENDERS
	40 min - Unusual clearance with the knee
	41 min 44 sec Long Ball
42 min 13 sec - Long Ball	

NOT MUCH POINT

There is no need to show you the whole game, because I can assure you nothing changes. This is as bad as it gets from a playing standard point of view. The solution to this second-ball game is to pick players based on their physical strength for what should be obvious reasons (the fight for the second ball) rather than for their skillful attributes.

THE FIRST-BALL GAME

There are a lot of misleading statistics coming to you from your television programs about the game you are watching. If you truly want to understand what kind of game you are watching, simply observe what the defense and the goalkeeper do when in possession of the ball. Here is an example analysis of what happens in a first-ball game. This analysis is from one of the most beautiful games I have ever watched, between Barcelona and Real Madrid. Barcelona at the time had the incomparable Messi and were managed by Pep Guardiola. This observation is focused on the actions of the Barcelona center half, Gerard Piqué.

Time	Actions
10 seconds into the game	Piqué receives the ball from the kick-off and takes a reverse touch, turning on the touch, and passes the ball to his goalkeeper. The goalkeeper plays the short ball out of his area and the ball is intercepted by a Real Madrid player, who attempts a pass which is deflected by a Barcelona player. The deflected ball lands at the feet of Benzema, who slots it past the goalkeeper into the back of the net. Barcelona are a goal down inside 20 seconds.

Observation: Will any of the Barcelona players resort to playing the long ball after the above goal scoring incident? Did the manager demand that his goalkeeper now change his style of play and play the long ball from now on? NO! Let us see how the game continues after the ensuing kickoff is taken.	
1 min 14 sec	A Real Madrid player tackles for the ball but doesn't get it. The loose ball ends up at the feet of Piqué, who takes control of the ball and passes to his left full back. Barcelona attacking possession results in a corner.
1 min 50 sec	Barcelona play a long corner, Piqué competes for the header, but the Real Madrid defense clears the ball. Piqué tracks back to his defensive position
3 min 20 sec	The Barcelona goalkeeper passes the ball between two Real Madrid players to his midfield player who is beyond them on the edge of his penalty box. The Barcelona midfielder knocks the ball across his own goal area to his left full back, who in turn plays the ball to Piqué to his right. Piqué takes a touch that enables him to play the ball to his right full back across the field in his defensive third.

The takeaway from this observation is that even when Barcelona had a difficult start, they did not resort to kicking the long ball. This first-ball game team endeavors to keep possession of the ball from the word go.

ON THE OTHER HAND

The observation taken from the second-ball game is clear. The second-ball game players of Real Madrid can't wait to get rid of the ball. No wonder though, keeping possession of the ball requires skillful play and if you are trained up to a second-ball game mentality, how are you supposed to be skillful, especially if your career from a very early age has revolved around a playing philosophy of getting rid of the ball.

OUTSTANDING

A first-ball game requires skillful players who know what skills to use and when to use them, when to keep the ball and when to release the ball. A player like Messi, for example, will use one set of skills when he finds himself in the middle third of the pitch and a different set of skills when he is in the final third of the pitch, especially when he is in possession of the ball close to the opponent's penalty area. Making the right choices in terms of what to do and where to do it depends on the ability of the player to implement the appropriate skills for any eventuality. Such a skills repertoire does not come from a forward-moving training environment. You need a first-ball game skills repertoire to be able to make things happen in the final third of the pitch.

CHAPTER ELEVEN

THE FIRST-BALL GAME

THE SKILLFUL APPROACH

I took the time to study the Barcelona game and recognized that this is a first-ball game, one that is based on keeping possession of the ball and so requires any number of specific soccer skills. I began my work on the first touch options for the first-ball game back in 1992. I realized that the reality for any player during a game of soccer lies in the fact that in different areas of the soccer pitch there are different skills that have to come into play. Some soccer skills are essential in some areas of the pitch and some not so much. This will always be the case because the game of soccer has two parts to it, the attacking phase and the defending phase.

IN THIS MODERN DAY

People often talk about their personal bubble. This is not as far-fetched an idea as you might imagine. In all events, including the game of soccer, players play the game within their own personal bubble. This is especially true when it comes to the first-ball game from a possession point of view. The start of any action begins with the ball at the player's feet. This reality requires specific skills, ones that enable the player to keep the ball close to his feet. This is why the player has to possess a wide range of first touch options, no matter what area of the pitch he operates in. Here are the essential first touch options that enable any player to keep control of the ball within his own playing bubble.

COACHING THE FIRST-BALL GAME – THE 360° PLAYING MENTALITY

STAYING IN THE PLAYING BUBBLE

The practice of the first touches you are about to see takes place in the 'Four cone' placement. The 'Four cone placement' is a simulation of the playing bubble around the player. The objective of the practice, therefore, is to work on the length of touch, which is trained in line with the most efficient use of space and time on the ball. A specific length of touch must be matched by a specific direction of touch. The first-ball game is based on keeping possession of the ball, which essentially means passing the ball to feet. The passes to feet are usually short (from 5 yds to 10 yds). In tight spaces, where there are opponents fighting for possession of the ball, the player needs to be at his best and possess a very good first touch to the ball. Keeping possession in a tight space means having the ability to take a meaningful first touch, one that keeps the ball close to the player's feet or one that moves him into an advantageous position and gives him the best possible options to either get away from any opponent or to make the next pass possible.

THE FIRST TOUCH OPTIONS

PLAYING IN THE BUBBLE - THE 360° FOUR CONE PLACEMENT FORMAT

THE FORWARD TOUCH

Player A1 stands within the four-cone placement as if he has his back to the opponent's goal and works on the forward touch to the ball. The forward touch is played with the inside instep of the foot.

Note – In relation to all the first touch options, the touch should never be more than 1.3 yards in distance. If the first touch relates to the most effective use of space, then the player taking the touch should always either keep the ball close to his feet or move with the ball and follow through on that touch to the direction of that touch. Some of the first touch options, like the above forward touch or the 'Set up' touch shown next, can be played to the front of the player, and be specific for a given purpose.

THE SET UP TOUCH - SETTING THE BALL UP

The most effective use of space inside the player's personal bubble requires a first touch that keeps the ball close to his feet and away from any threat to possession. In keeping possession of the ball, there are always going to be time constraints and tight spaces, which is why the first touch must be precise. Setting the ball up opens the angle to the side of the player for playing the pass short.

Note – It is important to appreciate the fact that such touches begin with the player developing the correct physical strength and the feel for the ball, which takes place first in the cone placement I have named 'The Nine Cone Placement' format.

MOVING THE BALL OFF THE LINE

Moving the ball off the line to the lateral angle is a touch option that opens the angle of play to the '180 degree' possibility to the front of the player. The objective of the practice is to pass the ball to the right or the left foot of the player, who works the ball from the center of the four-cone placement. There are lots of technical considerations here. The development of a first touch to the ball has to be fit for purpose, so naturally in a first-ball game scenario, the purpose is one of keeping possession of the ball. So, the ball must be passed with accuracy and just the right amount of strength, enough so that the power on the ball can be utilized to create the next game type solution. This type of first touch can come into play when the receiving player has little time to spare, or just long enough to lift his head and see more of the game.

THE EXTENDED FOOT TOUCH OPTION - A VERY FLEXIBLE TOUCH

A TWO-FOOTEDNESS CAPABILITY

This first touch option, which is also played with the inside instep of the foot, is like a key that unlocks everything. I call this 'The Extended Foot Touch'. In the most proficient of players, this out of the body inside instep foot touch has huge possibilities in terms of the direction of the touch, because the ball can be played out of the body to more than just the 45° shown.

NOTE –The extended foot touch, played with the left foot or the right foot off the player's half turned position, can move the ball to almost any angle. It simply depends on the player's ability.

THE REVERSE TOUCH – THE TURN AROUND

The four-cone placement keeps the player focused on playing the first touch to a specific angle, one that gives him the best angle outlet against any defensive position. I have named the above first touch 'The Reverse Touch' because it is the opposite of the 'Forward Touch'. The player cushions the incoming pass with the inside instep of the boot and turns around on the touch to follow the path of the ball.

THE ROLL TOUCH AND TURN

The roll touch is similar to the out of body touch. In this touch option the foot is out-turned on the touch and the ball is played with the outside of the boot.

This roll touch enables the player to turn effectively against any opponent who invades his bubble and is marking him tightly from behind. Touch and turn against the body of the marking opponent to move beyond the defensive position.

NOTE – Any first touch to the ball can be played to any length away from, across, or even to the side of the player's body, but always to such a length that he does not lose possession and keeps the ball in his personal playing bubble most of the time. The practicing player working the ball from the center of the cone placement (The working bubble) has enough room to practice working with the ball to a 1.3 yds length of touch.

CHAPTER TWELVE

TO THE OUTSIDE OF THE PLAYER'S BUBBLE

IN FREE SPACE - 1V1

The game of soccer involves some 720° of angles on the field of play, but only exceptional players can ever hope to play every first-ball game touch to all the directions possible. The most common standard of play in the world of soccer is based on the 90° angle, which is most likely played to the front of the player, which meets the second-ball game standard. The sum total of all the first touch options represents a 360° capability.

THE HORSES FOR COURSES MENTALITY

Proper player development should move away from the forward-moving mentality and recognize that the game of soccer has moved on and is made up of many parts, the most important of which is based on a proper first touch and a proper repertoire of skills, ones that enable the player to deal with any first challenger for possession of the ball. When it comes to coaching young players, there should never be a blanket solution. Many coaches profess to know about the game but prefer to know nothing about the soccer pitch or what it means in terms of player development.

ENFORCED IDEOLOGY

The game is forward-moving, they say, which is an excuse for creating a blanket solution to everything. The second-ball game does not concern itself with the development of the player to play with any quality within his own personal bubble, or with the type of skills required to play outside of it. Keeping players in a structured game ensures a lack of development. Lionel Messi, on other hand, who was never restrained by those who promote the big and strong players in preference to the second-ball game, learned the difference between the skills he needed in his personal bubble and those required outside of that bubble.

PLAYING IN THE DIFFERENT ZONES

The art of taking a first touch to the ball should not be confused with any one on one skill. Take a look at the soccer pitch diagram. There are different skill requirements in any of the sections on the field of play. It's not the same everywhere. Take a closer look at what happens in the different zones, consider the effects of the angles in play. Consider what takes place in the different zones. What happens in a game scenario where the players have stopped a counter attack and have won the ball back for the team in the defensive third. During a first-ball game the defense plays the ball out from the back with accurate passes because that is the safe option of how to play out of the defense, only in extreme danger does any player launch the ball out of this area. In the second-ball game, the defense behaves completely different, they don't pass their way out from the back of the defense but simply launch the ball as far from the defensive third as is humanly possible, especially the goal keeper. A second-ball game player is never comfortable playing the pass to get out of the defense area, but then how can he be, when he spent all his life kicking the long ball.

A DIFFERENT REALITY ALTOGETHER

IN THE OPPONENT'S DEFENSIVE THIRD

In teams where the skills are limited to the forward-moving mentality, players are designated to their functional roles. There are no requirements to employ a different set of skills for any particular area of the game. The attacking side of the game is left to runners and crosses into the opponent's penalty area. Such requirements have given rise to what is known today as the functional role. In other words, when the game is based on crosses of the ball into the opponent's penalty area, this requires a battler type player who can get his head on the end of such a cross. In England we saw players named Crouch and Davis who specialized in such a role.

THE FIRST TOUCH – PLUS - ONE ON ONE SKILLS

When the first-ball game players play the game of soccer everything is different, there are very few functional realities in such a team, especially when the team advances into the attacking third of the pitch, this is the area where the ability to go past defensive players uses the first touch options and the one on one ball control skills, all of which hold the key to any goal scoring opportunity. The following examples are out of the bubble skills, in other words, skills that are added to the first touch options that enable the player to avoid any challenge for possession of the ball.

Note - The development of two-footedness takes place automatically by the set tasks in hand. Anyone that plays skillful soccer will understand the work shown here. This next example is a volume of touch format, that ensures the correct development of the muscle memory and the strength in the overall leg position to work the ball in this combination of foot to ball manner.

THE PRACTICE OF 'ONE ON ONE' SKILLS

A TWO FOOTED COORDINATION FORMAT

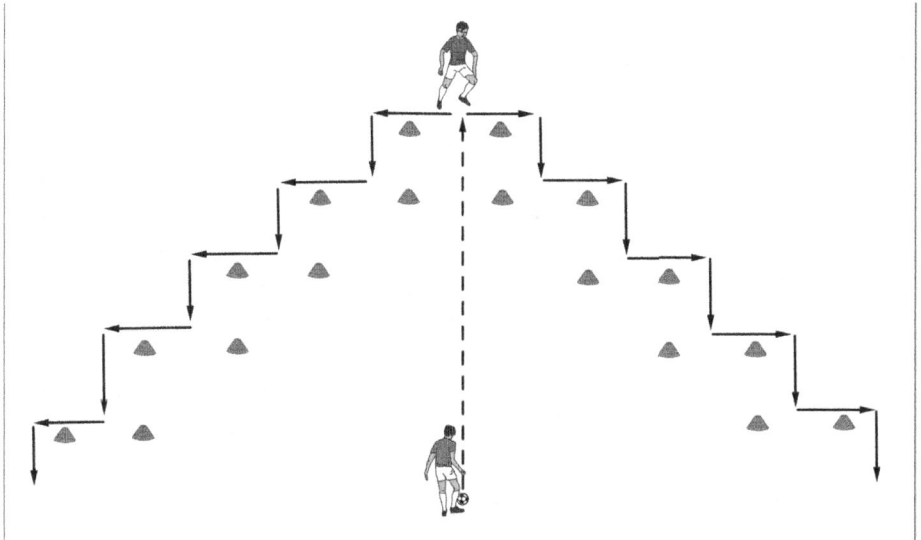

THE SIDE TO FORWARD STEPS FOOT TO BALL COMBINATION

See the following example of the physical movement combination. In Part 1 of this diagram - player A1 uses the inside instep of the right foot and moves the ball short to the lateral angle left and then uses the left foot to move the ball to a forward direction, thus avoiding the challenging foot. Sometimes when the player on the ball is confronted by a close opponent (something to be avoided) this is what he will have to do to avoid the first challenger's foot, and even the foot of any covering player, in which case he can double up on the lateral to forward touches of the ball as in Part 2 of the diagram.

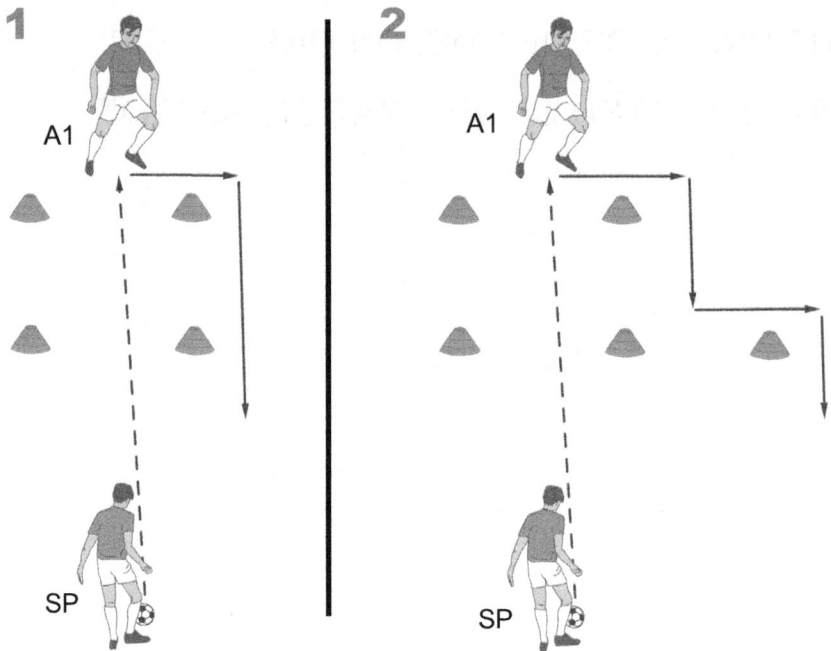

IN THE OPPONENT'S DEFENSIVE ZONE

This shape creates the right amount of work required to ensure the development of the fast twitch muscles and the reaction and therefore the physical ability to coordinate and use both feet to avoid a loss of possession.

NOTE – We have made it possible for you to see such action in a DVD titled 'Soccer Training - Developing the 360° Player'

Both the right and the inside instep of the left leg are involved in moving the ball out of the way of the challenging foot.

From a practice point of view, the service player can pass the ball and immediately move in to challenge A1. A1 avoids the challenge by moving the ball out of the way, with the right foot moving the ball to the side and the left foot moving the ball forward.

Cone placements – Set to shoulder width

Many of the 'ONE ON ONE' skills in a game of soccer require the player to combine the use of both feet in a coordinated manner. If the player is not in a position to be 'Two footed' then he will find it difficult to combine the use of both feet to the ball, in which case he cannot perform effectively in the attacking third of the field without the risk of losing possession of the ball.

KEEP UP THE PRACTICE

THE DOUBLE BLUFF

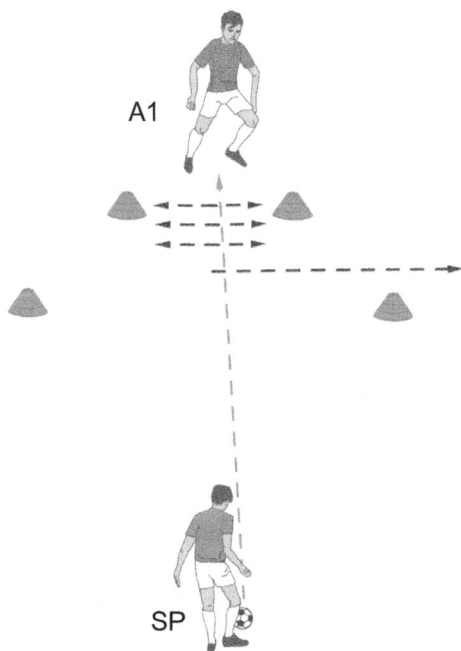

FAST INSIDE INSTEP TO OFF THE LINE TOUCH

This example is called 'Double Bluff'. Player A1 takes a number of short inside instep touches to the ball with either foot to move the ball through the practice gate and then once through the gate, he moves the ball off the line.

Note – For practice purposes you can have the player that feeds the ball follow his pass and act as a challenging defender. However, be careful to make sure that it's a passive challenge, not one that takes the focus away from the skill which is being worked on.

Note – The foundational development for the first touch and the one on one skills takes place in the 'Nine Cone Placement' – See DVD 'Soccer Training – Developing The 360° Player'.

ANY PHYSICAL WEAKNESS OF THE PLAYER?

All things being relevant, when the player is strong on one side, he will have no problems moving the ball to the strong side. So even a strong right footed player will have no problems moving the ball to his Left - handed side because the short touches to the ball are always performed with the leading foot. If the player is right footed, it is the right foot. If the name of the game is to develop a player that can move the ball to the 180° – 360° to the front or back of his position, then the 'Square on' ability and the two-footedness of the player is essential, this goes without saying. To be a skillful first-ball game player, the player has to have the ability to work the ball to both the right and left side of his square on physical position.

DEVELOPING MOMENTUM

When the attacking player takes on any challenging opponent, he needs to have quick feet and a fast, reactive brain capacity. The formats are specific to all of that. These forms also develop the muscle memory for the one on one skills. Such a muscle memory enables the player to perform any number of foot to ball touch combinations. In technique playing terms the player with the ball at his feet can solve any problem off the first touch.

PRACTICE PLAYING THE COMBINATION OF THE OFF THE LINE TOUCH WITH THE INSIDE INSTEPS SINGLE BLUFFS

This is what muscle memory development is all about and what we as coaches should employ in our training sessions. Only in this type of format is it possible to control what is essential to the player without wasting The player works to develop the ability to work the ball to the right and left of his position. This format also makes it possible to work on the fast feet movements, while making sure that no side of the physical being dominates the action over the other.

A COMBINED SOLUTION

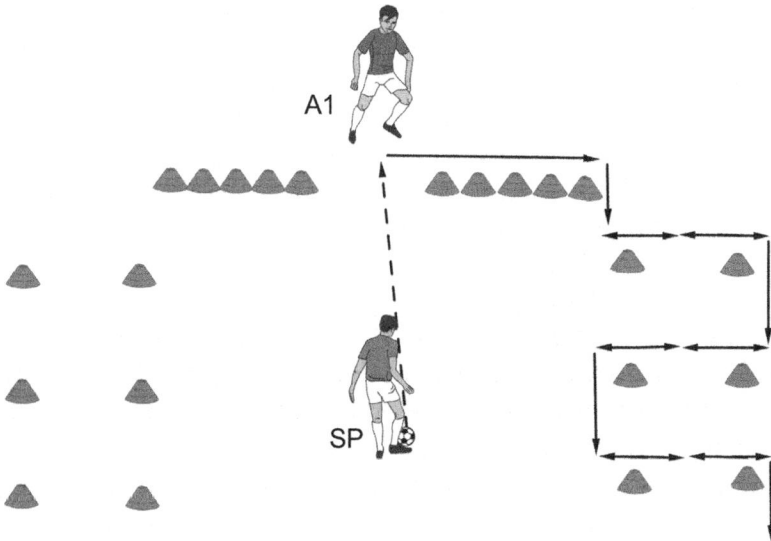

THE LATERAL IMPLICATION

THE DEFINITION OF SKILLS

It is never a question of taking anything away from any player regarding his/her ability to improvise, when required. That kind of thinking is not the issue here. The issue here is about developing a solid first touch base that can actually underpin any reality. Having said that, keeping possession of the ball requires the player to be precise with his choice of action. When the player lacks ball skills this does mean having to take lots of extra touches, which at times can be of little value and even worse, the player can lose possession of the ball.

OPENING UP THE AREA OF PLAY - LOOKING UP

The lack of such playing skills influences the decision process. It makes it more difficult for the player to know when to keep the ball or pass the ball, which means mistakes will happen all the time. This can contribute to the loss of momentum in the attacking phase. We can eliminate lots of such problems by making sure that neither side of the physical being dominates the other and the action taken will always be one that creates more opportunities in the given area on the field of play. The practice formats will always ensure not only the development of 'Two-footedness' but a much greater range of playing skills. I've mentioned the off the line touch many times before, but for me it's worth going over it again. This touch is unique because it is possible to move the ball off the line on receiving the ball or when already in possession of the ball, from within the playing bubble. In many respects it is an 'Anti' Second-ball game touch. Moving the ball off the line changes the playing angle and so can also move the ball against any defensive position. Any team that uses the off the line touch when facing the opponent's defense is hard to defend against because it can open up the area of play to 180°. In particular, any type of zone defense would be in trouble. Also, moving the ball off the line enables the player to develop the ability to see more to the front of his position and if he has a two-footedness, capability, he can move the ball to any direction, not just to the forward direction.

SOMETHING YOU RARELY SEE - THE DINK TOUCH OPTION

THE SKILLS IN USE

Imagine player A1 moving the ball off the line against the first challenger and then coming out and being challenged by a covering player D2 and with no time to spare having to avoid the second challenging foot, he dinks the ball over that challenging foot, problem solved. All examples here develop the ability to link up with different touches to the ball that then enable the player to move the ball against any number of challengers.

INCLUDING A DINK TOUCH

Player A1 can first move the ball off the line to open up the angle, then take a forward touch to the ball and then, if a challenging foot appears, dink lift the ball over the challenging foot. When 'Dinking the ball' (against the second challenger's foot) the ball is lifted off the ground with the toe down but also with laces part of the boot. Such work requires perfect balance, hence the need to work the ball with either the left or the right foot. In the interest of developing the correct physical balance, the player is also instructed to work the ball as is shown by the above example but the starting foot next time around in comparison to the above example, would be the left foot. The 'Dink Touch' is obviously a useful skill to have in any tight situation. Maestro Messi one of the best players in the world also includes this type of skill in his playing repertoire of skills. The first-ball game is about skillful play, so why not make it playful and fun and effective at the same time.

LATERAL VS FORWARD-MOVING

Working the ball to a lateral angle forms a strong foundation for all the first-ball game skills, including the One On One skills. When it comes to the soccer pitch, there are 720° of angles that can relate to the game of soccer, but only a handful of skillful players around the world can ever hope to play to even the 360° possibility. Most commonly, the game is based on the 90° angle, which forms the second-ball game mentality. The first-ball game, at its best, requires a 360° mentality, a mixture of 180° to the front and back of the player. Why? Because the first-ball game is not just a forward-moving game. So 90° if it is a second ball, forward-moving game with unskilled players – 180° if it is a first ball, forward-moving game – 360° if it is a first ball multi-directional game. Of-course none of this makes any sense until you understand the implications that stem from the lateral input forms and what they means from a playing point of view. When Messi played for Barcelona, he could easily play to the full 360° angles on the field of play.

THE LATERAL INPUT

The reason for the lesser abilities in many players today is simply down to what is worked on at the practice ground. The development of the skillful player should include lateral work on the player's 'Two-footedness', the proper first touch options and 'One On One' skills. Such endeavors cannot be achieved in any drill type solution, which is often based on nothing more than a simulation of the second-ball game. What you see are coaches working on free kicks and crosses, as if that's going to raise standards. The 'One On One' skills, just like the principles of defending, require special working solutions.

CLARIFY

SHARING Possession is much different than KEEPING possession. I myself am guilty of using the phrase "possession game" when talking about the first-ball game. But I worry that it gets misinterpreted as "KEEPING possession" rather than what I really mean, which is "SHARING possession". The pundits who promote the second-ball game often refer to the first-ball game as 'keeping possession for the sake of keeping possession'. However, the true aim of the first-ball game is to efficiently find solutions all over the pitch and ultimately create scoring opportunities by sharing possession as opposed to hoofing the long ball (essentially giving up possession) and hoping to regain it in a 50/50 situation. That for me is the difference!

CHAPTER THIRTEEN

THE SKILL OF PASSING THE BALL

I have seen coaches work on the art of passing the ball by having players facing each other twenty yards apart and simply kicking the ball to each other. I have seen players form a circle and pass the ball to each other, while one player is in the middle offering token defense. This circle thing is often used as a warm up, a so-called routine before a game of soccer. None of that is any good! You can't develop the ability to pass the ball or to receive the ball effectively by lining up the players some 20 yds apart and have them kick the ball to each other. The circle idea is also not worth a carrot, because it probably does more harm than good. Far too often the skill of passing the ball just happens and the players either have the ability to pass the ball or they are just about adequate.

FIRST THINGS FIRST

When it comes to developing the ability to pass the ball, the most important of considerations must be the development of physical strength in the groin area and the lower abdomen. In addition to this strength development, the player needs a strong foot position, which is often to the out – turned inside instep foot position with the toe pointing down to the ball. The pass from this foot position is called 'The Push Pass'. The half-volley is played with the toe down and laces to the ball. Yes, it is possible to have two players standing a short distance away from each other and make them pass the ball all day long or stand in a circle and knock the ball about or leave it to just the playing side of the game and see if that improves anything. Leaving things to chance is not a serious attempt to development passing skills.

NOTE – When the players help each other in all the working formats, this too contributes to the development of the ability to pass the ball to feet. However, there are serious issues that need to be worked on in addition to the practice of the pass to feet, for example:-

THE AGILITY FORMS

THE GROIN STRENGTHENING FORMAT

Nobody would think that an agility exercise has anything to do with passing the ball, but they would be wrong. This agility work should be included in any meaningful training session on passing skills. Special agility (specific movement forms) of work strengthens the player in the groin and abdomen area of the body, not to mention the legs, the foot etc. This agility work has the best effect on the physical body when it comes to developing balance and strength.

SWEEP JUMP OVER AND BACK AGAIN

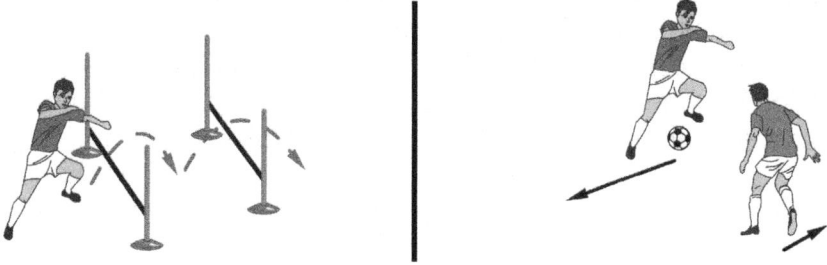

ADDITIONAL BENEFITS

A deliberate change in the working pattern between the simple jump overs at the center of this format and the sweep overs with the one foot leading performed on either side is actually very difficult to do. This is because the work is based on kinetic tension, which is generated by the variation in the type of movement experienced and therefore very effective when it comes to creating the correct conditions for developing strength in the required areas.

NOT ALWAYS NECESSARY

Sometimes these development solutions have a better effect on the physical side of the player than any weight training routine. These are movement forms of training that are specific to the needs of the game. In the above format we can get the player to work on the higher levels of stamina (on the development of the inner core strength) straight away by simply employing the use of his own body weight. It is surprising what the players own body weight can do when the work is movement based. In this format, simply moving the body to the lateral angle over the tapes is enough to tax the player and since the body reacts to effort, you can imagine what this means. This type of work strengthens the legs and gives the player the inner core strength to strike any ball with the right kind of quality.

THIS SHOULD NOT BE THE NORM

In a second-ball game, you rarely see any player move the ball on with the first contact. You will not see a one-two played anywhere.

First, the player with lesser ability takes a stop touch to the ball, then a second touch and then another touch. Anyway, they simply can't move the ball on to another player on first contact off a pass. In many cases, the lack of ability to do so is a result of some genius who thought, "I know! I can improve the player's skills by conditioning him to take two or three touches to the ball before he passes to another player". Good idea? No! This has nothing to do with player development, it is there to dumb the game down for the purpose of creating the second-ball game. All my working solutions end with a pass to a working partner or partners. I have never conditioned players to take just two touches (contacts) to the ball.

HOW TO WORK ON PASSING SKILL
THE PASS AND MOVE OBJECTIVE

PASSING – DEVELOPING POWER & TECHNIQUE

LET'S GO THROUGH THIS WORK - STEP BY STEP

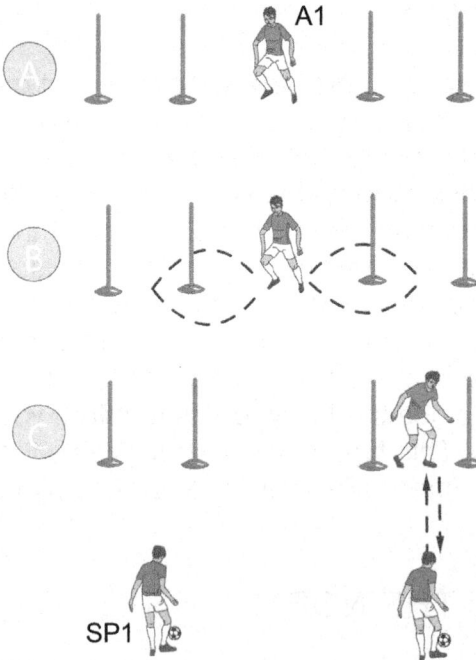

Sharing possession is based on passing the ball to another player, which requires the development of some seriously important skills. To put it another way, the first-ball game is not based on the player's functional role but instead on creative physical movements that are supported by the pass. The step by step breakdown of what takes place in each format describes how to work on the pass and move skills. The player works the format to a figure 8 running pattern which is specially designed to bring him through the sticks in an upright physical position.

(a) This shows the starting position for the player working on the pass backs to player SP1 and SP2 – passing the ball with the inside instep of either the left or the right foot.

(b) This describes the physical movement to the figure eight pattern - development of the pass and move habit.

(c) This shows the input into the practice format from both players – SP1 and SP2. The job of the service players is to serve the ball to the practicing player – SP1 passes the ball to the right foot of player A1, SP2 to the left foot. This is to develop the ability to pass the ball to the right or the left foot, which is necessary in situations where the ball needs to be shielded from an opponent.

WHY THE FIGURE EIGHT WORKING MOVEMENT PATTERN?

Getting into the right habits is a matter of development. In practical practice terms this movement format creates the upright approach to the ball, which enables the player to not only move correctly to the ball but practice applying the out turned correct foot position of the inside instep of the boot/foot to the ball with a good follow through to the direction of the pass. Getting into good habits includes moving off the pass, hence the figure eight movement.

THE ANGLED PASS

A pass can be played to the 720° possible. In other words, it can be played to any angle. To achieve this, the player needs to develop the pass with the out-turned inside instep to the ball and the pass made with the toe down laces part of the boot. Interestingly enough, the ability to pass the ball short is easily done with the inside instep foot out-turned position, whereas the more difficult passes of the ball, to a wide range of angles, require the player to develop the toe down and laces part of the boot to the ball.

LACES TO THE BALL

In the next example, the player works on moving the ball to a diagonal angle with the laces part of the boot, passing to the inside of the service players SP1 and SP2. By inside, we mean to the left foot of SP1 and to the right foot of SP2. SP1 and SP2 must make sure that they pass the ball to the outside of the stick when the player comes around in order to keep the player moving without a hitch. The timing of the pass is coached here, because SP1 and SP2 have to make sure that the timing of the pass relates to the practicing player's movements. If you look at the above format, the figure eight run of the practicing player does not come through a gate. The run is simply done to the outside of the stick. This enables the player to pass the ball with the toe down laces of the boot to a diagonal angle.

THE DIAGONAL PASS

LACES OF THE BOOT TO THE BALL

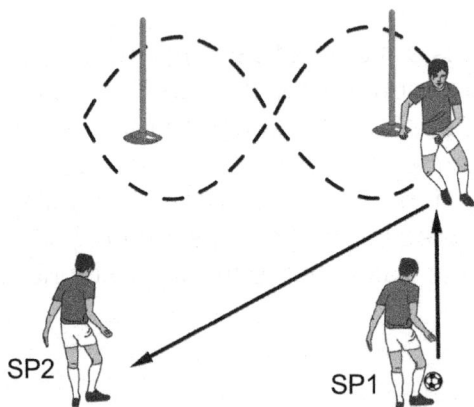

THE FIGURE EIGHT PRACTICE SEQUENCE

In this type of format the players develop the correct habits automatically. There is no time to admire the pass back to the service players because after passing the ball back to SP1 the player will have to make his way quickly to the other side of the format to receive and pass the ball back to SP2. The habit of not admiring the pass is part of the training experience. The ability to work the pass backs in the above format is obviously dependent on the player having a 'Two-footedness' capability. The balanced physical requirement should be clear, because if the player is weak on one side of his physical being, that reality could cause all sorts of problems.

CHAPTER FOURTEEN

A CHANGING MENTALITY – MAYBE!

THE EMERGING GAME

At least here in England, thanks to a Manager called Pep Guardiola, the first-ball game is alive and having good success. There are different ways of playing soccer, true, so the choice is there. I chose to teach the skills that improve the players ability to play soccer. To what level is always going to be down to either the effort put in through practice or the opportunities to play for a soccer club that represents a certain standard. The choice is always there, or at least it should be. Unfortunately, the world of Soccer is a mixed bag of realities, where there are those who deny opportunities to young people regarding their development for different reasons. The 'Horses for courses' mentality is one, another is the support for the second-ball game, which I call a cheat in many ways because there is not much to it and is covered by the good old saying professed by the second-ball gamers themselves, as 'Money For Old Rope' –

NOT IN THAT RESPECT

I played the game at a time when there was very little commercial interest. In fact, all we got at times was our expenses (lunch money). I loved playing soccer in the midfield, where I could create the pass and move skills that ended up in a goal scoring opportunity. Scoring goals always gave me a buzz that I will always remember. This is why I began to take an interest in coaching players back in the nineties and it wasn't long before I realized that something was amiss. I concluded that most of what happened to the coaching side of the game after the creation of the English Premiership in 1992 came from decisions that had their roots in Nationalism here in England, and not always from any consideration that the coaches would have even thought of. I know it is difficult to comprehend that political decisions influence how the game is coached, but that is how things sometimes work, especially in circumstances where money is involved. What does supporting the second-ball game amount to if not a specific form of discrimination based on Nationalism? Sometimes, we have to go the long way round to get to the truth. What changed and how the changes came about in recent times is more than revealing. Allow me to take you back to the point in time when I believe the many vested interests interfered with the game and as a result, the emphasis of the coaching changed from developing skillful players to selecting players based on physical size and strength, which has influenced the game right up to this very day. This is the year 2022 and the English game is still biased towards the second-ball game.

MY SOCCER COACHING PHILOSOPHY

My own coaching philosophy was born on the back of the realization that financial considerations played a big role in what took place on the training ground. The resulting physical approach to playing soccer began to take place just after 1963/64 under the watch of Sir Alf Ramsey. I believe that what Ramsey did to the way team England played was the beginning of the end of the skillful player. Under Ramsey, England was able to win the World Cup in 1966, but the consequential fall out effect of the changes that he made to the way he set out his players on the pitch 4 – 1 – 2 – 3 was significant after that period of time. In copying Ramsey's team shape, the coaches of that time gave birth as it were to the team shape known as the 4 – 3 – 3. I can't imagine for one minute that the people in charge of the game back then (THE ENGLISH FA) understood the dire consequences that the 4-3-3 team shape would lead to, because if they did know, then this was the beginning of the anti-skill soccer endeavors that led to the corruption of the game on behalf of vested interests.

THE DOWNSIDE

The consequences of a system that did away with the skills side of the game came home to roost when some of the richest people in the world became the owners of Soccer Clubs. The top clubs no longer hired the second-ball game player. The problem of a lack of first team opportunities for the home grown players came to a head when the English FA tried to negotiate with the top clubs to provide opportunities for English players and not side-line them out of the first team, as was the case in England during the 2015 season, where only a handful of home grown players took part. How ironic is it that in 2022 the players are taking a knee regarding all forms of discrimination, while there are clubs that do practice discrimination in one form or another.

THE LEVELING OUT SOLUTION

The influence on the playing standards comes from all sorts of different factors such as the ability of the individual, the quality of the coaching and so on. Now I am not going to baffle you with science here but the decision by Sir Alf Ramsey not to have wingers in his team and to play to a forward-moving direct attacking style meant that he in effect began to eliminate an essential ingredient from the game of soccer – laterality.

NO LATERAL THINKING

THE DEMISE OF THE FIRST-BALL GAME

The forward direct style (no laterality) required a different type of player from one that used the entire field of play. Opening up the lateral dimension allowed players the license to be more individually creative and much more able to interact with other players. How could a lack of laterality possibly matter to the game of soccer? A more interesting question for me is whether the notion of laterality is known to the people that govern the game of soccer. I ask this because the working principles of laterality are seriously important to many things in our lives, not only the game of soccer. Laterality is a function that describes the physical reality that most people experience. For example, the use of the right hand rather than the left hand. When people develop the use of the right hand, they naturally develop the left side of the brain (the left side cerebral hemisphere) – more so than the right side. We know this because it is the left side of the brain that works the right hand. The word laterality and therefore the lack of laterality means that everyone who is right handed or one handed is predominantly weak on one side of the body and when it comes to the sum total function of the brain it is also said to lack collaboration. In other words, the left side dominates the right side of the brain. Under such circumstances, the sum total of the make-up of the brain doesn't work together as a single unit, hence no collaboration and no laterality. The major implication of a lack of laterality when it comes to the game of soccer is that most who take up the game will also kick the ball with the right foot. When Sir Alf Ramsey implemented his direct line of attack policy on the style of the England team, he in effect enforced the laws against lateral thinking. The lack of laterality made it possible for him to get the players to play to his requirements, which we know to be based on his forward-moving mentality.

THE COACHING IMPLICATIONS

ENFORCING THE LACK OF LATERALITY

When it comes to soccer, the lack of laterality makes it possible to keep the game under control, not only from a playing point of view but also from a player selection point of view. A game played to the forward-moving mantra requires a more physical type of player. Both the lack of laterality and the forward-moving mentality have had their consequences to this very day. When the game is dominated by right footed players with no lateral ability, the playing standard is controlled by two major factors;-

(a) Coaching The Forward-moving Mentality
(b) Ignoring the lack of laterality (two-footedness)

THE CONSEQUENTIAL REALITY

The system of development that keeps the players using the "one good foot" ignores the many issues involved with the missing coaching principles that fall under the concept of laterality. There is little reference to the lack of 'Two-footedness' in the coaching of players. The lack of understanding laterality is the root cause that sustains the status quo in coaching today, where certain attitudes prevail and the continuation of bad coaching solutions are sustained in the name of a Horses for Courses solution and the second-ball game. The resulting forward-moving game has become the playing mantra of the people who support the consequences of the forward-moving mentality, which creates the second-ball game effect.

THE RIGID DESIGNATED POSITIONS

PLAYING THE GAME TO THE STRIKERS

The 4 – 4 – 2 playing system enables the managers and their coaches to control the game more effectively because it allows them to dumb the game down by implementing conditions on all the players to, for example, keep to their designated roles and to their given positions in the team. This system is not an accident of evolution, it is a playing system that caters for the commercial interests now in the game where money interests dictate every-thing. Some owners of the top clubs in the English Premiership are more interested in commercial activities and expect the Man-ager to create a team where the strikers are highlighted. Think of players like Harry Kane and Wayne Rooney. The rest of the players on the team were encouraged/instructed to work the ball to the designated striker/s at all costs and as directly as possible. Obviously in the name of commercial interests.

AT THE GOVERNING LEVEL

When everything is controlled, even down to the youth levels of the game, most of the training solutions have to conform to vest-ed interests, hence some training solutions do not actually come from the coaches themselves, but are ordained from the powers that be at the Club.

THE SMALL SIDED GAME

A PUBLIC RELATIONS EXERCISE

One of the most blatant lies ever told to young people interested in playing soccer was that 'The small sided' game is the best in-vention since sliced bread and the place to develop soccer skills. The truth was and is different. The small sided game is simply a bad copy of the real game and as such it is a very different game in many respects. This was simply a solution to the lack of facili-ties, popularized by the media and given the name "five-a-sides". The five a side was a fast track solution, nothing more, nothing less. To begin with, it was a question of a lack of facilities for chil-dren to play soccer. Just as with the creation of the forward-moving game, in the form of a second-ball game mentality that had its consequences to the skills side of the game, the same thing applied when the powers that be introduced the five a side idea. Did anyone think about the game of soccer from any point of view other than commercial interests when they introduced the Small Sided Game? The priorities for the local council and for the business world were business orientated and money motivated. It had nothing to do with any concerns about the needs of the children and their development as soccer players. Nobody cared whether the small-sided game was good, bad or indifferent. Just like the functional role in any game, with its forward-moving reality, the small sided game was never the place to develop many of the technical and physical requirements for any skillful game of soccer.

EVERYONE CAME ON BOARD

The five-a-side became a coaching solution that had all the ingredients for the second-ball game. This was no place for developing the real skills of the game, those relevant to the first-ball game. Anyone that copied this solution ended up with players that are second-ball game orientated.

NOT JUST IN ENGLAND

Like soccer missionaries, English coaches traveled abroad to preach the second-ball game mentality to neophyte soccer countries in places like Africa and North America. Often through a work program called BUNAC, English coaches flocked to spread and share their "expertise" to players and coaches hungry for knowledge and training ideas. Armed primarily with their second-ball game philosophy and a cool accent, these coaches had an influence on the soccer cultures of these nations that persists to this day, particularly in the USA.

THE FORWARD-MOVING GAME

IN THE FINAL THIRD - FEED THE BALL TO THE STRIKER

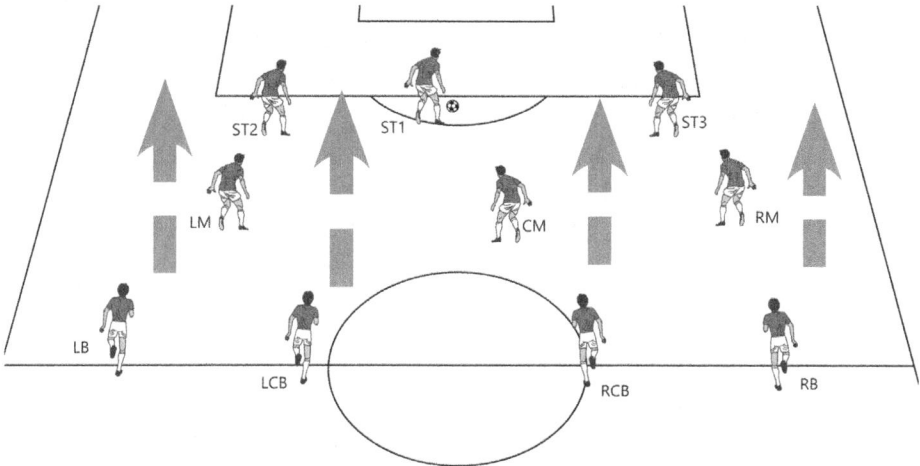

No wonder ex-players like David Beckham jumped on the gravy train and to earn their living in America by plying this kind of philosophy. America is stuck in a second-ball game reality and hasn't won anything major at the Men's Senior Level. All that has happened in America, and in England for that matter, since the year 1966 is the enforcement and promotion of a coaching philosophy that supports the existence of the second-ball game.

A SUMMARY OF THE GAME

It seems to me that the whole world (except Spain) bought into what was in effect the demise of the skillful player. The manipulation of the game on behalf of vested interests began with the creation of the English Premiership in 1992. It was not long after that that the owners of the big clubs realized that in order to win titles, they would need to bring in the best players from around the world. Bringing players in from all parts of the globe did raise the playing standards in some teams and teams like Manchester City did benefit from bringing in foreign players, but this also resulted in changes to the way the game was played. The downside to this reality is the disparity in the playing standards at all levels of the game. This disparity happens because not every owner of every club has the millions to spend on quality players. What we have ended up with in England, and indeed on the continent of Europe, are three types of soccer. We can say that we have the first-ball game, the second-ball game and the hybrid game. The easiest of games to coach and play is the second-ball game. The second-ball game in its pure form is based on the big and strong player and on a forward-moving mentality that does not rely on high levels of skill, but on battling attributes and the long ball solution, especially when playing the ball out of the defense. The long ball game is designed to cause lots of battling for the ball (fights for the second ball) to hide the reality of a lack of first touch and relevant first-ball game skills.

THE FIRST-BALL GAME

The first-ball game, on the other hand, is made up of quality players in every position of the team and the game is based on the concept of 'pass and move'. The first-ball game players have a functional role but are not shackled to any structured game. When it comes to the make up of the first-ball game team, therefore, we can say that there is little disparity between the players in terms of their individual abilities and the game is predominantly played on the ground, where the ball is shared, and the long ball is not played unless it is absolutely the only option open to the defense.

IN A HYBRID GAME

Oddly enough, there is a compromise solution, in the form of a game known as 'The 'Hybrid Game' This game results from having a mixed bag of players that balance out between the skillful and the battling type of players in the make-up of the team. This mix of players with different abilities creates a game that can fluctuate between the skillful game (the pass to feet) and the long ball game. This type of game exists because the procurement of players is done on the basis of financial implications and not on any opinion as to whether the player coming in is compatible with any requirements. Such a situation comes about as a result of the owners of the club making deals on players. This is known as a buying and selling club. Not the best of clubs to work for.

CHAPTER FIFTEEN

JUMPING ON THE GRAVY TRAIN

If a player wants to compete at the highest levels of the game it is his/her skill level that dictates what can be achieved. Not tactics, not team shapes, nothing. What really matters is the quality of the player. There is nothing that can't be changed or adapted to, but it is a question of attitudes. Is it a coincidence that the big clubs go for players from Latin America? I don't think so! I believe that children in a warmer climate will experience a different lifestyle, one that will favor the development of the fast twitch muscles. Does that mean that those not born in warmer climates cannot develop into great players? Of course not! Any good coach any-where on the planet can use the knowledge that human beings are made up of slow and fast twitch muscles to figure out how to develop players. The information is out there. We know that the slow twitch muscles work with oxygen (aerobic) and the fast twitch muscles do not use oxygen to function (anaerobic). This is consequential to the development of any human being. We know that under normal circumstances, the predominant muscles in use are the slow twitch muscles – We also know that when a person engages in physical effort that stops him from taking in oxygen at a comfortable rate, he can be said to be in an anaerobic state and that effort is most likely focused on the fast twitch muscles. Many of my working formats develop and therefore engage the fast twitch muscle forms, which in terms of development is specific to the requirements of the first-ball game.

THE IMPLICATIONS

It is interesting how a country like the Netherlands has benefited from their bicycling culture. Children in that country cycle every-where. Because bicycling aids in fast twitch muscle composition, it is not an accident that the Netherlands has developed numer-ous world class soccer players. In other countries, like England, where bicycling is common, for many reasons, it's a different sto-ry. Very few children in England bicycle and so may well not have the opportunity to experience the anaerobic state (a fast twitch state). Not only that, but there exist factions in England that want to limit the role of physical education and sport in the schools.

THE INFORMED REALITY

GIVEN DIFFERENT ENVIRONMENTS

My point is that in every country of the world, things can be as different as chalk and cheese. The bridge between all soccer playing countries can actually be based on the lateral development concept. There are no good reasons for that not to be the case. It is my belief that human beings begin life with a strong inner core (a much bigger ratio in favor of fast twitch muscle) no matter where they come from and that is one of the reasons why children in general can't sit still. I believe that the muscle composition ratio between the slow and fast twitch muscle groups can be changed as the years go by depending on the lifestyle and training activities experienced. Activities that promote normal oxygen intake to take place, like sitting down in a classroom, watching television at home, playing games on a computer and eating too much carbohydrates and, get this, even playing lots of five a sides in a cold climate, can promote the development of slow twitch muscles because the slow twitch muscles function under aerobic conditions and obviously will grow bigger if targeted consistently with aerobic activities. The consequence of this is lesser technical ability.

SERIOUS CONSIDERATIONS

It is simply wrong to ignore such issues and shove everything under the table of the forward-moving mentality. When it comes to the type of game played, there is a choice open to everyone. It is possible to control the work ratio between the aerobic and the anaerobic state of being to achieve the all important difference of choice. Any worthwhile objective should be based on the ratios of work between the slow and fast twitch muscle forms. The ratio of work set between the two variants in the muscle composition makes all the difference as to what a human being can turn into physically. If you think about the game of soccer, you will realize that the skillful side of the game requires the fast twitch muscles, which can only be developed with formats that have the ball at the players' feet.

IN ADDITION TO THE ABOVE REALITY

There exist outside pressures on the development of the human being that anyone interested in player development should also take into account.

NEGATIVE INFLUENCES:

1 – Carbohydrates – The effects of a bad diet– Eating a lot of chocolates – cakes – sugary laced foods etc – Eating carbohydrates is not a problem if the energy produced by such foods is used straight away. The problems come from not using the energy stored that such foods produce. Any excess energy from sugar based substances is stored as fat cells, mostly on the outer core of the physical being. Hence the big and strong appearance, which is good for the second-ball game but not for the first-ball game, for rather obvious reasons.

2 – In some developed countries, children spend long hours in a school environment. Sitting down for long periods has a low energy level requirement and any intake of food in a sedentary environment such as this is again stored as fat, which can be seen on the outer side of the body – abdomen – bottom etc.

3 – Functional Training that fails to promote the anaerobic state to any meaningful effect. Burning less energy means storing energy.

4 – Obesity – It is not how much food is consumed as opposed to when it is consumed. Everyone tends to eat at the wrong times, like for example, in the evening when watching television or just before going to bed. In such circumstances there is no requirement for energy to be spent in young children and so the excess energy is stored around the body.

I am not at all surprised that children in some developed countries are constantly exposed to environments that make them heavy set and less mobile. If most of the physical activities do not touch the base of the anaerobic state (getting out of breath) and the children continue to eat and stay in the aerobic state all day long (easy breathing patterns) then this will most certainly promote the development of slow twitch muscles. Whether in England or America or anywhere on the planet, the problem of development is the same for everyone. Nobody has a monopoly on the development of any player. Players are human beings, not robots.

CLEARLY NOT SO!

The game of soccer is not one that is down to opinions, but one that has its links to a soccer-specific scientific approach. It is wrong to suggest that the composition of the muscle is set for life genetically speaking. If that was the case, it would simply be impossible to play golf or soccer or snooker or any other such sporting endeavor for that matter. If the training is wrong from a muscle composition point of view, the slow twitch fibers will always dominate the fast twitch fibers, simply because of how the body generates energy from the glycolysis process which uses oxygen. When it comes to any sporting endeavor, the composition of the muscle must be changed with development in order to be fit for purpose, which means that the training concept has to favor the fast twitch muscle form if we are talking about the skillful game of soccer known as The First-ball game.

THE PATHWAY TO SUCCESS

It is possible to have a working principle that actually makes all the difference.

Number one is the development of the muscle composition in the human being to be fit for purpose. This is a working principle related directly to any chosen activity.

Number two, closely related to number one, is the need to develop the 'Muscle Memory' that can perform any chosen activity. These two major pathways to success go hand in hand. It is no surprise that players trained up in the five-a-sides would have inherent problems when playing the proper game of soccer. One major consequence that is widely ignored is the reality that even the most famous players in the world are essentially one footed. Some of them are so weak on their "off" foot that it prompts comments such as, "He's only got the one good foot, the other is for standing on!".

THEN WE HAVE THE INFLUENTIAL PUNDIT

Ex-professional players comment on soccer games on television. Millions of people watch and listen to what they have to say. Whether intentional or not, much of their commentary can be misleading. One such misleading example relates to the touch taken to the ball. When a player receives the ball from another player, the pundits talk about the touch to the ball, making comments such as 'That was a good first touch'. Funnily enough, they don't often comment on a bad contact with the ball. Sometimes I feel like educating the pundits, because when it comes to any first contact with the ball, there is a lot more going on than what they say about it and some of what they say is actually misleading. Some comments are not helpful, especially to youth soccer players. When players receive the ball from a pass, the first contact on the ball is very rarely a proper first touch. Unless they are trained in the first touch options, more often than not they are simply stopping the ball at their feet and then taking another contact to put themselves in the best position for a subsequent action. With a proper first touch, this second touch is unnecessary, as the player has already assessed and set himself up in the best position with the one appropriate first touch. Most players don't have a first-ball game skills repertoire and so you see them make sometimes two or three contacts with the ball before moving the ball on with a pass to another player. Many players play the game to a conditioned habit, one that was developed on the training ground in the conditioned game of two or three contacts to the ball. When you watch some games, it is clear that the players have been instructed to make two or three contacts to the ball and then pass the ball. The pundits then say, "What wonderful skills this team has, just look at how they play two touch soccer!". Neither the pundits nor the players know any different. So, pundits and players alike, allow me to describe what a proper first touch on the ball is. What I describe below is a real first touch option, one that every player should have in his repertoire of skills.

THE PROPER FIRST TOUCH TO THE BALL

1 - Taking the ball Off the Line – Taking the ball off the line is taking a touch with the inside instep, moving the ball across the body. If the player is two footed, then he can obviously move the

ball to the right or left of his body position and can face any direction on the field of play.

2 - The Set Up Touch – This is a touch that is played to make the ball sit up nicely for a pass. The 45° angle of touch makes the ball more playable for the longer pass options

3 - The Extended foot touch – This is an incredibly useful touch to have because it can take the ball to a 180° options angle of play on the right or the left side of the player's body. The inside instep of the foot to the ball is applied, but rather than taking the ball across the body, it is moved out of the player's body to any direction of play he wishes on contact with the ball. If the player is two-footed, he can virtually cover a 360° angle in play.

4 - The Dink Touch – The dink touch is taken to the ball with the laces side of the boot toe down. This touch is useful in tight situations where the opponent arrives at the feet of the receiving player just as the ball does. The ball is simply lifted over the opponent's challenging foot and out of his reach.

5 – The Forward Touch – The forward touch simply takes the ball to the front of the player. The most common use of this touch is moving the ball forward on a run.

6 - The Roll Touch – The roll touch is a touch on the ball that sends the ball around the corner to the back of the player receiving the ball and his marker. Using the outside of the boot, the player sends the ball to the back of his marker, turns on this touch and moves after the ball.

7 - The Stop Touch – The stop touch is self-explanatory. It is a touch that simply stops the ball at the player's feet.

8 – The Reverse Touch – When the player has his back to the opponent's goal he can take the ball on the inside instep and turn on that touch.

Can you imagine the possibilities of a two-footed player employing the first touch repertoire to solve playing problems, not to mention the repertoire of One On One skills.

CHAPTER SIXTEEN

THE GENERAL SUMMATION

I don't believe a good coach should ignore the first-ball game skills that I have been discussing in this book. Many of them know that there are a lot of things wrong with the one-footedness of the player because everyone either laughs about it or simply ignores it. Even the most famous players get away with their inability to play the ball with either foot and that is because the game of soccer can hide any reality, especially if on television you have a commentator that ignores lots of these things during a game.

NOT OPTIONAL

At the very outset of any young player's career, the approach to his development should be based on a game of soccer that encourages players to play the ball out from the back. This will allow each player more time on the ball than can be the case when the player is exposed to a forward-moving experience and the second-ball game. In other words, the training environment should be skills orientated and based on a two-footedness approach, not on the one-footedness approach that exists because of the training ratios and lifestyles that favor and therefore promote the use of the one good hand and the consequential use of the one good foot. Also, players should not be forced to play in a strict functional role or be expected to win games by an aggressive physical presence, which is very often the expectations of any coach that has a second-ball game mentality. Far too often at youth levels of the game, winning a game means more than the players' development. I believe it is the coach's responsibility to look after the interests of the players and their futures. If this results in winning games, great! But winning should never be the main priority of the youth coach. It is absurd for any youth coach to think about winning games as opposed to thinking about the development of the young players in his charge. The youth side of the game should not be controlled by the expectations of the baying crowd or the bosses of the youth club or Academy. One of the biggest crimes against the game of soccer is the de-selection of talented players in preference to the big and strong player because he gives the Academy a winning hand. How many players do you see coming through the system as a result of bad attitudes or vested interests in such clubs? The answer is, very few! Anyway, we are where we are and I think it's time to take the problem of a lack of 'Two-footedness' seriously. If we do, we can raise the standard on the playing side of the game for sure! The implications to the youth side of the game are simple enough, the choices are simple enough. Since it is impossible now to legislate against the business reality, there is a need to change the system at youth level, which includes the way the game is coached. Everyone should remember that the game of soccer is in competition nowadays with other sporting endeavors and it is all too easy to lose the support of the people.

MY FINAL SUMMATION

USE THIS FORMULA

DEVELOP THE TWO-FOOTED PLAYER = THE PASS AND
MOVE GAME = THE FIRST-BALL GAME = THE 360° PLAYER

THE LATERAL INPUT IMPLICATIONS

We can argue till the cows come home about all sorts of reasons why things are the way they are. Possibly the pressures on coaches from above, possibly the lack of funding, possibly God knows what, but when all the dust settles the truth is simple. I believe in producing players of a high quality and in order to achieve this there is no choice but to select players on the basis of talent and to develop that talent in a training environment that does not shirk away from the reality of a lack of two-footedness but actually embraces the need to work on and develop a two-footedness ability with a multi directional approach to playing soccer. There is no other way, not if the game is to stay prosperous in the future.

THEY WILL NOT CHANGE

I am not an enemy of good coaching ideas, but the business interests that exist on the back of the youth side of the game that have sprung up since 1992 have done very little for the home-grown players in terms their development. How can anyone, for example, profess a soccer skills approach to the development of the player when they have been an integral part of the fraternity that supported the second-ball game since 1966? The development of the young player must take place within a training environment that is directly related to the physical movement forms that are based on the choreography of the proper game of soccer. The most skillful game of soccer known today is the first-ball game, and this game is not a forward-moving game. It is a game based on a first touch skill repertoire, backed by the ability to play effective one-on-one skill solutions to any direction, with either foot. Two-footedness combined with a full repertoire of skills creates a 360° player, capable of sharing possession of the ball. Remember that even a great player like Messi never hesitates to pass the ball to a teammate who is in a better position than him to create a goal scoring opportunity. Players who have this 360° capability are rare exceptions in today's game that is still dominated by the forward-moving mentality and all its implications.

IN CONCLUSION

The game of soccer is unlike any other sporting endeavor in the world. Most of the soccer clubs in England, for example, are deeply rooted in history and tradition and therefore are embedded in the social fabric of their communities. Strangely, though, the supporters usually have very little say in how the club is run. It is this fact of life that can be abused by those who happen to be in charge. The other side of this reality is the power of money. In today's reality, money dictates everything, especially when it comes to delivering on the supporters' expectations. I have seen the business side of the game and this can be the most complicated unsolvable problem for many clubs, especially where the expectations of the supporters do not match up with the club's means to deliver on expectations. I have been there, so I know what the problems are all about. The development of young players should be kept separate from the business at the professional level. In other words, youth players should be independent of any concerns related to the first team of any professional soccer club. There should never be a horses for courses mentality involving the development of any young soccer player. By horses for courses I mean grooming young players to serve the needs of a particular level in the game. The development of young players should be based on the best coaching concepts, ones that will ensure the interests of the player and not the interests of any business surrounding the professional game which has its many problems. Yes, there are the so-called divisions in the game, between the second-ball game and the first-ball game, but as far as I am concerned the development of any young player taking up the game of soccer should be based on the first-ball game, pure and simple. That is my opinion!

My hope is that with this book I have managed to have stirred up the coaching pot somewhat and that at the very least I have given some useful points of interest to the coaching side of the game. I have tried to be objective and have simply told it like it is!

Made in the USA
Middletown, DE
24 September 2022